YOUR TOWNS & CITIES IN WORLD WAR TWO

DEVON

AT WAR 1939-45

YOUR TOWNS & CITIES IN WORLD WAR TWO

DEVON

AT WAR 1939-45

DEREK TAIT

Pen & Sword
MILITARY

First published in Great Britain in 2017 by
Pen & Sword Military
an imprint of
Pen & Sword Books Ltd
47 Church Street
Barnsley
South Yorkshire
S70 2AS

ISBN 978 1 47385 575 5

A CIP catalogue record for this book is
available from the British Library.

Printed and bound in England
By CPI Group (UK) Ltd, Croydon, CR0 4YY
Typeset by Aura Technology and Software Services, India

Pen & Sword Books Limited incorporates the imprints of Atlas, Archaeology,
Aviation, Discovery, Family History, Fiction, History, Maritime, Military, Military
Classics, Politics, Select, Transport, True Crime, Air World, Frontline Publishing,
Leo Cooper, Remember When, Seaforth Publishing, The Praetorian Press,
Wharncliffe Local History, Wharncliffe Transport, Wharncliffe True Crime and
White Owl.

For a complete list of Pen & Sword titles please contact
PEN & SWORD BOOKS LIMITED
47 Church Street, Barnsley, South Yorkshire, S70 2AS, England
E-mail: enquiries@pen-and-sword.co.uk
Website: www.pen-and-sword.co.uk

Contents

Chapter 1:   1939 – The Outbreak of War   7

Chapter 2:   1940 – The Battle of Britain   31

Chapter 3:   1941 – The Blitz   60

Chapter 4:   1942 – Run Rabbit Run   118

Chapter 5:   1943 – Over Here!   136

Chapter 6:   1944 – D-Day   160

Chapter 7:   1945 – Victory   182

              Acknowledgements   198

              Bibliography   198

              Index   199

1939 – The Outbreak of War

The rise of Adolf Hitler and the Nazi party, together with tensions in Europe and the spread of fascism in other parts of Europe, ultimately led to the start of the Second World War. When Germany invaded Poland on 1 September 1939, outrage was felt across the world. Great Britain and France declared war on Germany two days later.

On the day Germany invaded Poland, teachers in Devon received a communication stating that due to the hostilities in Europe, all schools would be closed until further notice. This gave time for officials to allocate places for children who were being evacuated from London which was seen as a major target. The West Country was thought to be a safe area for them to be housed.

At the same time, lights all over Devon were turned off and a compulsory order was issued to prevent home owners from allowing any light to be seen from outside their premises. The order also applied to businesses and shop owners who had to turn off

A barrage balloon flying over Plymouth. Many were stationed in parks and gardens and provided a defence against an attack from the air.

any illuminated signs as well as lights in their windows. Motorists were required to fit regulation masks to their headlights. With the general feeling that the conflict would escalate, there had already been a great demand for black-out material, so much so that shops soon ran out.

On 3 September the Prime Minister, Neville Chamberlain, announced the outbreak of war on the radio. In Plymouth large barrage balloons were floated above the city in anticipation of an enemy aerial attack. On the afternoon of 3 September, 800 schoolchildren arrived at North Road Station in Plymouth.

The general mobilisation of armed forces began and the National Services Act was passed by Parliament introducing National Service for all men aged between 18 and 41.

An order was issued to stop people gathering in large crowds which meant that places of entertainment such as cinemas and theatres were closed. The few people who had television sets found that the BBC had stopped broadcasting for the duration of the war. Memories of the First World War were still fresh in the minds of many residents in Devon and most knew what to expect.

A warning was issued which stated:

Keep yourself off the streets as much as possible; to expose yourself unnecessarily adds to your danger. Carry your gas mask with you always. Make sure every

Women wearing gas masks in Mutley, Plymouth. In September 1942, a mustard gas demonstration was held. The area was roped off to the public and later cleaned up with bleach. However, a day later, two boys played in the area and developed mustard blisters and had to be rushed to hospital.

member of your household has on them their names and addresses clearly written. Do this on an envelope or luggage label and not on an odd piece of paper which may be lost. Sew a label on children's clothing so that they cannot pull it off. People are requested not to crowd together unnecessarily in any circumstances. Churches and other places of public worship will not be closed. All day schools in evacuation and neutral areas in England, Wales and Scotland are to be closed for lessons for at least a week.

Meanwhile in London, according to the *Daily Mirror* between two and three thousand American refugees left the city during the night. Many were destitute. An American Embassy official stated that it might take ten days before there would be sufficient ships to evacuate them all. Joseph Kennedy, the American Ambassador, appealed to all American and other neutral steamship companies to provide available ships, including freighters and tankers, to aid with the evacuation.

On 4 September the new central recruiting offices for Devon were opened at the Castle Street Congregational Rooms in Exeter. Recruits were signed up for the Army and Air Force. Other facilities were to be arranged for the Royal Navy and Royal Marines. 'The keenness to join is remarkable,' stated Major F.R. Logan, the zone recruiting officer.

Army recruiting offices continued to function at Barnstaple, Torquay and Launceston.

The *Western Morning News* of Monday 4 September carried a story under the headline GERMANS IN DEVON:

'I have no idea what will happen to German subjects who are living in Devon and Cornwall, as I have had no instructions from the German Embassy,' said Mr S. Carlile Davis, German consul at Plymouth, to the *Western Morning News* yesterday.

Sandbags being placed in position outside Barnstaple police station.

'There are a few Germans in Plymouth in domestic service and in training positions. Some of them have gone home on their own accord, but I have heard nothing of the matter. Many former Austrians, now German citizens, are living in the Torquay area, and I know at one time within the last year there was quite a colony at Yelverton.'

Mr Davis said he had no knowledge of any German shipping being in the port of Plymouth.

An order was issued allowing the armed forces to take horses in North Devon for use in the war. Banks closed for the day while they took time to complete measures to deal with the emergency. They opened again for business on 5 September.

Adverts were placed in newspapers asking people to take in child evacuees. The response was very good although some were not keen to help. A local newspaper reported that a few householders who had so far been unwilling to receive evacuees were asked not to force the government to exercise compulsion. Sir Warren Fisher, the North West Regional Commissioner, pointed out, 'It is not possible at present to say how long the billets will last. But all must be prepared for danger and hardship and will be lucky if it takes no worse a form than receiving strangers into one's house.'

Householders who billeted evacuees were paid ten shillings and sixpence for the first child and nine shillings and sixpence for each additional child.

On 5 September the National Registration Act was introduced which decreed that all residents of the UK would have to carry ID cards.

On 6 September it was reported that gas masks were more generally being carried in Exeter, although the percentage of people in the city, as well as in Exmouth, who took the sensible precaution, was not as high as it should be. Respirators had been issued to all members of the Devon Constabulary and the Exeter City Police and from 7 September all police officers on duty were required to carry their gas masks.

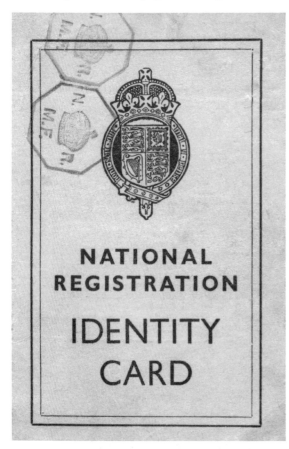

NATIONAL REGISTRATION IDENTITY CARD

A National Registration Identity Card. National registration was introduced in September 1939 and during wartime everyone was issued with a card which they had to carry at all times.

On Thursday 7 September, the *Western Morning News* reported on a shortage of members in the Land Army and appealed for women to join. The article stated that already the great exodus from the land had begun. Men were leaving the fields to take up arms for their country. Women of the West Country were expected to carry on in their stead. The Women's Land Army recruited anxiously and, it was stated, Devon and Cornish women had made a poor response to the calls for recruits. Devon had enrolled 380 members and aimed at securing 7,000 women and girls for land work. The host of evacuees in the area were setting a shining example to those with whom they had come to live. Several had joined forces with the Land Army. Like the rest, they enrolled either at their local employment exchange or with the district representative of the Land Army.

Torquay led the way in providing volunteers for Devon. Plymouth and Exeter were doing their fair share of providing recruits. However, there was difficulty finding sufficient farmers to train the girls and it was said that unless many more farmers offered to co-operate, and thousands, not just hundreds of women answer the call of the Women's Land Army, there would be a tragic tale to tell at the time of the winter harvest.

The *North Devon Journal* of Thursday 14 September reported that local residents were taking things calmly:

North Devon's position is best summed up in the words of a woman refugee from London. Walking through Barnstaple High Street on Thursday, she commented, 'You wouldn't think they knew there was a war on in North Devon. People

Members of a Plymouth based naval ship practise gas mask drill.

A poster used to attract women to join the Land Army.

seem to be taking things so calmly.' At no time has North Devon shown signs of alarm or anxiety to any great extent and the effect of the emergency in its early stages on business generally is now giving way to steadier buying and selling. The demand on the provision shops has eased off considerably.

Rehearsals for an attack from the air took place in Plymouth. Colin Campbell, the Town Clerk, was appointed Air Raid Precautions Officer and anti-aircraft batteries were set up together with barrage balloons and air-raid sirens.

Almost a quarter of all shop staff in Plymouth enlisted in the services leaving many under-manned.

The *Western Morning News* noted that Plymothians were more careful regarding their gas masks than many people in other places, where the number lodged at the lost property offices had been considerable. During the first week of the war, fifteen respirators were left on Plymouth corporation trams and buses and these waited to be redeemed at the Milehouse depot.

The *Western Morning News* of Friday 15 September carried an article about householders in Plymouth being fined for not screening lights.

Three people were fined two pounds each for being the occupiers of premises where illuminations were not properly obscured under the Emergency Powers (Defence) Regulations restricting lighting. Mr W.E.J. Major pleaded guilty on behalf of Mrs Edith Vera Gray of 1 Sturdee Road, Devonport. Constable Thompson stated that at 9.15pm on 7 September, the defendant had the door of her shop at Sturdee Road, open. A bright beam of light shone across the road. He asked her to shut the door, to which the defendant replied 'you had better stop and shut it for me.' Mr Major pleaded for leniency, saying his client had tried to buy black-out material to make a curtain for the doorway but had been unable to do so. She had since managed to purchase some and the light was properly obscured.

Elfred Lee, of 8 Duke Street, Devonport, a shipwright in the dockyard was summoned for having lights showing from the windows of his home. He was asked to switch them off by Constable Gibbs and said that he would do so presently. Lee pulled the blind but it did not obscure the light. Lee said that he did not realise that a candle would show through a blind. In the case of Alfred Mason, of 23 Pier Street, Plymouth, Constable Hill stated that he knocked twice at the home of the defendant. On each occasion a light was showing through the window. It was extinguished following his knock but switched on again shortly afterwards.

During September, every member of the Exeter branch of the British Legion was doing his bit for the country. Their chairman, Brigadier General W.F.S. Edwards, told the *Western Morning News* that many of their members had been summoned to act as special constables, ARP wardens and a number were joining up with the Defence Corps Company. Also, those on reserve had been called up. He pointed out that owing to the voluntary duties that they had already taken on, many were not in a position to offer their services in the fighting forces, while others were over age.

Some members who were Reservists had been called up for active service, and others had enlisted for different kinds of special duties. All were over the age of 45 and those who had taken up ARP work were mainly around 60. It was added that the women's section had shown a readiness to step into the breach caused by the absence of the men in a perfectly loyal and helpful manner.

On 16 September, petrol rationing was introduced. There were substantial supplies of the fuel in the country but in the national interest, it was felt that these must be put to the best use. It was announced that there would be no change in the price of petrol at least for fourteen days.

One of the first tragedies to hit the region was the sinking of the locally manned HMS *Courageous* which was torpedoed by a German submarine on Sunday 17 September leading to the deaths of 519 crew members. The ship, which had left Devonport on 3 September, was the first British warship to be sunk by Germany and fell victim to *U-29* commanded by Captain Lieutenant Otto Schuhart.

The *Western Morning News* of Saturday 23 September carried an article on people's worries about their pets during the war. It mentioned that Plymouth animal lovers had adopted the slogan, 'wait and see' and had not hurried to have their animals destroyed because of the war.

Mr F.W. Slee, who was in charge of Mr T. Darton Deeble's Infirmary for Dogs, said that he had had an unusual number of inquiries on the Sunday that war was declared as to whether it would be most humane to bring their animals to be 'put to sleep' or to take the risk and keep them. He managed to persuade the majority of owners to wait for at least a week and had been inundated with letters of thanks for his advice.

Towards the end of September, lorries were requisitioned to assist the ARP and other vital services. This meant that many stores had difficulties delivering their goods to customers, an expected service during peacetime.

The *Western Morning News* noted that a Torbay area National Defence Company had been inaugurated with headquarters at Torquay, which was met with a most encouraging response, particularly from ex-servicemen. It was commanded by Captain H. Tracy Barclay, chairman of the Torquay British Legion. One of the difficulties experienced was that older men were so anxious to serve that some had given ages considerably below what they really were in order to come within the limit.

Sports of all kinds were affected during September and there were many abandonments. One headline read SHORTAGE OF PLAYERS AND BAD WEATHER. It went on to say:

The international situation and heavy rain combined played havoc with sport in the West Country on Saturday and, except for the more important league matches, few football engagements were carried out, clubs finding it impossible to get together full teams.

The Government had forbidden all sports where crowds were likely to assemble and league football ceased. Although the day was set for the opening of the rugby season there were no matches played in the west and Plymouth Albion abandoned their practice game owing to the shortage of players.

The Emergency War budget was introduced by Sir John Simon on 27 September. As well as petrol rationing, a duty was placed on whisky which was expected to raise an extra £3,500,000 a year. The tobacco duty and sugar duty was also raised. The latter led to an increase in the price of jam, marmalade, tinned fruit, syrup and sweetened milk.

On Thursday 28 September the Devon County War Agricultural Executive Committee announced that the War Office had agreed to a further extension whereby soldier labour might be available to assist farmers where civilian labour was not available.

An article in the *Western Morning News* suggested how luminous paint could be used during the blackout. However, people had made inquiries to obtain the paint but only one of the six firms visited in Plymouth had stock at the outbreak of war. When buyers were asked how they intended to use the paint some said they would paint electric light switches and cupboard doors. One or two shopkeepers, aware of the difficulty of the public in determining at night whether a 'blacked-out' shop was open, considered painting the word 'open' in front of their premises in luminous paint. It was asked whether hostile aircraft would see the paint outside. A man in the trade thought there was little likelihood of that; he thought its cost would militate against extensive use, particularly on large-scale projects.

During September, it was announced that 6,366 women had enlisted, in the south-west region, for the Women's Voluntary Service for Civil Defence. The area included Devon, Cornwall, Somerset, Dorset, Gloucestershire and Wiltshire. This brought the total recruitment for the year up to 32,182.

Identity cards were introduced on 30 September.

By the end of September, over 82,000 evacuees were housed in Devon.

On 1 October, the call-up proclamation stated that all men aged 20 to 21 must register with the military authorities.

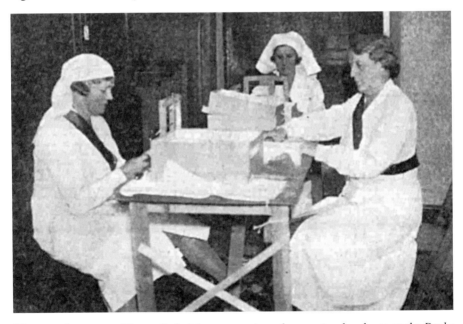

Women volunteers at Plymouth, knitting garments and preparing bandages at the Drake Street War Aid Supply Depot during October.

At the beginning of October, it was announced that nearly fifty members of the Territorial Army Nursing Service were engaged in work at a military hospital 'somewhere in the West Country'. They were reportedly delighted with their surroundings and had shown particular interest in the scenery of the district saying that the hospital was ideally situated. Recruiting for the service had taken place in peacetime when the majority of nurses joined. The two matrons in charge had been taken on at the end of the First World War. The nurses were from all over England but the majority had come from Birmingham.

The *Western Morning News* of Monday 9 October reported that shopkeepers were regularly asked, 'Have the candles come in yet?' Invariably the answer was 'No!'

Large stores were finding that all their customers inquired hopefully after candles. One manager stated that customers wanted a few candles just in case the electricity was cut off. Six leading grocery stores were completely out of candles and they were not able to give any of their customers an assurance as to when new stock would come in. One manager said, 'We ordered twenty cases of candles and six weeks later we received two.' This was the general state of affairs.

In some shops when rumour spread that stocks had arrived, it attracted would-be candle buyers like honey attracted bees. One woman was walking along Russell Street when she saw a queue outside an iron-monger's shop. 'What are they queueing up for?' she asked. 'Come along my dear,' said one kindly soul, 'the candles have come in.' The candles sold out in three days.

'Four Feathers', starring Ralph Richardson and John Clements, was shown at the Gaumont in Exeter during October 1939.

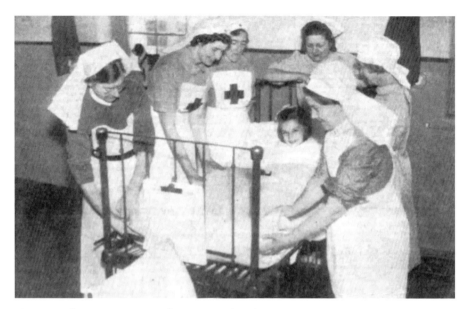

Nurses under instruction at the Prince of Wales's Hospital at Greenbank, Plymouth, during October. Five members of the Royal Auxiliary of Civil Nursing Reserve assist in bed-making.

On 21 October, registration began for men aged between 20 and 23 to be called up for National Service. People who were exempt from the Act included the medically unfit, students, clergy, conscientious objectors and people working in reserved occupations such as farming, baking and engineering. The call-up had a severe effect on many firms and some small businesses had to close down.

Some people seemed unhappy about the colour of the sandbags scattered around Plymouth as mentioned in the *Western Morning News* of Monday 23 October. Plymouth at present only had the ordinary-coloured sandbags some of which had been painted white. Unlike Liverpool, it did not sport any gaily hued ones to brighten up the streets. One man who wanted to see coloured sandbags in the streets was Mr L. Duckett, the principal of the Plymouth School of Art.

'Actually I quite like the appearance of the sandbags as they are,' he said, to a reporter. 'However I think colouring them would be a good idea. For one thing if the canvas were treated with paint, this would act as a preservative and the bags would last longer. For another, the large masses of bags there are in some spots could be camouflaged by being painted in different colours, such as pale yellow and dark red. In addition, I do think painted bags would brighten up the appearance of the city and have a cheering effect on people. If they were painted, I think good startling colours should be used and not any dull, drab shades.'

Alderman S. Stephens said that if sandbags were painted it should be done at the minimum expense. In his opinion, it would be better if they were kept clean and white, to enable people to see them at night. Mr E.S. Leatherby said he did not think

Promptly at noon on Saturday 21 October 1939, the first batch of men, between the ages of 20 and 22, registered at the Plymouth Employment Exchange, under the National Service (Armed Forces) Act, 1939.

Men eager to enlist at the Plymouth Employment Exchange during October 1939.

there was any specially good purpose to be served by having coloured sandbags if the idea was to simply brighten the streets.

In October it was announced that the firework celebrations on 5 November were unlikely to go ahead. Although fireworks had already appeared in the shops, it was felt that these should be saved to celebrate the eventual Allied victory and also that it would be impossible to let off fireworks without infringing the lighting laws. Furthermore, it was forbidden to let fireworks off in the street and there was a War Emergency Order controlling noises; sudden loud noises might scare people who were worried about a possible air raid.

During October, Warner's Holiday Camps at Seaton and Paignton were used as internment camps for aliens living within the area. The camps housed Jewish refugees, Germans, who had escaped the Nazis, as well as German nationals and supporters of the Nazi party.

The *Western Morning News* of Tuesday 24 October reported that the war was causing hard times for window cleaners saying that they had been affected to some extent by the blacking-out of windows, Mr E. Whitmarsh, manager of the Three Towns Window Cleaning Company stated that a number of business premises had closed, other premises, including public buildings, had their windows partially blacked-out and other windows were protected by sandbags. Asked if employees had been affected by being calling up, Mr Whitmarsh said none of them was liable for service at the moment, although some would become liable if the military age was increased to 44. Several of the firm's employees were auxiliary firemen, and had proved useful, as they were used to working on ladders.

'We employed some women in the last war, but they were not a great success,' said Mr Whitmarsh, when asked if the firm was considering the employment of women. He continued, 'Climbing ladders was not woman's work.'

It was reported towards the end of October that Plymothians had thoroughly blackened out all of their windows and that they were buying large quantities of black-out material. There was an excessive demand for material and paper to darken windows and an increased demand for the better, heavier type since they were introduced in dark green, brown and blue, as a variation from the usual and gloomy black. Spooners and Co in Plymouth noticed that customers were asking for more colourful designs. There were many ingenious designs of electric light shades, the most popular one shielded the light from the vicinity of the window and allowed its full radiance to shine over the remainder of the room.

During October, the Jewish community of Plymouth, centralised at the synagogue, made their contribution to the war effort. The Rabbi, the Reverend W. Wolfson, said that the women of the community were assisting the lady mayoress in services and meeting daily at Stonehouse Town Hall and the synagogue. Refugees in the city were willingly assisting in sewing and knitting. There were thirty or forty refugees in the city from European countries to whom the war had brought hardship and uncertainty. Among the number were twelve German Jews who were being supported by charitable donations. Unable to work for the time being, they were all desirous of appearing before an aliens' tribunal as soon as possible so that they could obtain employment in some form of national service. They were not allowed to be supported by public funds and were being cared for by the Plymouth branch of the National Jewish Women's Committee.

The *Western Morning News* of Thursday 26 October carried an odd story which read: 'If a German woman possesses two pairs of summer shoes she is not allowed to buy a new pair of winter shoes, according to a German broadcast yesterday.'

The paper started the 'Empty Stocking Fund' in an effort to raise £200 for Christmas presents for poor children. Collecting cards were issued at Leicester Harmsworth House in Frankfort Street. The directors of Spooners donated £2 10s while the staff donated £2 2s.

At the beginning of November, the Lady Mayoress of Plymouth (Mrs G.S. Scoble) made an appeal on behalf of the War Aid Supply Depot at Stonehouse for people to assist with sewing, knitting, helping out in the surgical room and with teas.

Lord and Lady Astor, of Plymouth, taking a stroll with some of the 83 orphans who were wartime evacuees at their Thames-side home.

She added, 'We are also collecting old clothing at the depot for fitting out shipwrecked crews. The clothing must be clean. The men sometimes landed with only what they stood up in. Some of them were clad only in dungarees and had not even a jacket. I would appeal if there are any of you who have any left-off clothing to send it along to the Stonehouse depot. About 400 men, women and children were brought in a week or two ago and I wish you could have seen those people and the gladness in their eyes when they saw the piles of clothing for them.'

On the evening of Thursday 2 November, the Women's Institute entertained the troops at Cullompton's Assembly Rooms. Under the supervision of Mrs Raven, the ladies catered for 300 servicemen. Farmers and friends brought gifts of apples and cigarettes and, after supper, Mr J. Jago presided over a sing-song.

The *Express and Echo* of Monday 6 November told the story of London evacuees living in Devon. It mentioned that two small twins from an evacuation area in London, who had been billeted in the house of kindly Devonshire people, were responding well to home training in unaccustomed surroundings. It continued that on one day, when dinner was over, the foster-mother said to them, 'Say your grace and then you may get down.' Brian obeyed but Donald remained silent and declined to leave the table.

'Why don't you say your grace?' asked his hostess. Donald spread out his forefinger and thumb. 'Because I've still got that much room left,' he replied.

This was one of a number of amusing stories told in a report compiled by a London schoolmistress in charge of evacuated schoolchildren who were attending a village school in Devon. The report, which surveyed the reactions of the children to their new surroundings, was read at a gathering of educationists at Barnstaple and was

Plymouth's ration books being carried by assistants from the Guildhall to GPO vans to be distributed throughout the city.

said to be 'a striking testimony to the happy way in which London kiddies in the county generally are responding to the real West Country hospitality and care of both teachers and the parents now looking after them.'

During November, Plymouth City Council suggested that there should be more white lines painted as well as kerb stones as people were finding it difficult to find their way about at night. Residents in Seymour Road, which was particularly poorly lit, painted their gate posts and pillars and suggested that if everyone did the same it would save the council a great deal of money.

The *Western Morning News* of Friday 10 November carried the story of marine Michael Davey who had escaped through the porthole of HMS *Royal Oak* after the ship was sunk by a U-boat in Scapa Flow. Marine Davey swam four-and-a-half miles before being picked up. Davey, from Axminster, had been a gardener before he joined up. It was reported that he was in his hammock when he heard the explosion in the fore part of the ship. Members of the ship's company went to investigate without realising that they had been hit by a torpedo. After about twenty minutes, there were three more explosions and the ship took a heavy list and the lights went out. Davey was reported as saying, 'At first I thought that we had been bombed. Fumes and nearly choked me. I scrambled to a porthole in the darkness and crawled it. By then the ship had listed to an angle of 45 degrees; by the time I got out had started to roll over. I don't remember jumping into the water at all. What I can remember was coming to the surface with a shipmate gripping me around the throat.'

After being rescued, Davey enjoyed fifteen days' leave at his father's smallholding at Monkton Wyld.

In November it was reported that firm friendships had been struck up between young Londoners in East Devon and local children as a result of several soccer games arranged by Mr J.J. Kleinman who was the sports master at Heygate Street School at Walworth.

In the second week of November it was decided at the annual meeting of the Devon Agricultural Association that the Devon County Show should be suspended for the duration of the war.

Lighting and blackout regulations fell, in some places, on deaf ears and the *Express and Echo* of Tuesday 21 November carried a report of a prosecution. For nearly four hours, an electric light shone from the doorway of Beacon House, Pinhoe, during the black-out period. According to evidence heard at Wonford Sessions, when Lady Hull was summoned for contravening the black-out regulations, the light could be seen for a considerable distance. Lady Hull, who pleaded guilty to the offence, said she switched the light on when a friend came to condole with her on the loss of a pet dog, and that a servant had forgotten to turn it off. 'Being tired, I went on to bed,' said Lady Hull, 'and my maid ought to have looked round the house to see that all the lights were out.'

PC Potter, of Pinhoe, said that he understood that Lady Hull, who had been up for two nights, was rather distressed over the loss of a pet dog.

Announcing that the summons would be dismissed on payment of costs, the chairman, (Mr G.T. Arthur) said it was the first case of its kind to come before the court.

In the *Western Morning News* of Wednesday 22 November, the Admiralty appealed for knitted items to be sent to men serving in the navy. Gloves, mittens, wristlets, pullovers, sea-boot stockings, scarves and balaclava helmets were all required. Instructions in the newspaper gave the sizes and colours that knitters needed to adhere to.

The *Express and Echo* of Wednesday 29 November carried a story about the WVS which stated that Devon women were co-operating whole-heartedly in the work for the Women's Voluntary Services for Civil Defence. Work parties were particularly active in making wallets for the ARP workers which included 26,000 sterilised dressings, bandages, scissors, tannic acid, iodine pencils and lint; 12,000 triangular bandages had also been made and 4,000 first-aid wallets had been provided for wardens with 269 for the police.

The Devon County WVS concentrated on working for the Navy League to provide comforts, and they were particularly anxious to carry out the work as quickly as possible as the need among Devon men was great. Clothing and boots for evacuated children was dealt with by Mrs Phillips, the county organiser, in conjunction with the Public Assistance and other organisations and in close co-operation with the LCC teachers.

At Newton Abbot, the centre organiser, Mrs Pope, was responsible for helping with blind people in the community. Three canteens had been established and there

Plymouth's women ready to extinguish any fire. Early tasks for the Women's Voluntary Service included evacuation and making medical supplies such as bandages (from old sheets), pyjamas and nursing gowns. In Feb 1939, with their roles ever expanding, they became the Women's Voluntary Service for Civil Defence although they were known more commonly as WVS.

were 600 workers and a social centre for troops. There were fifteen teams of canteen workers, as well as two teams kept in readiness for helping should any wounded arrive at Exeter.

The Exeter centre was active in a variety of ways since the outbreak of war and during the evacuation period. The transport section had been particularly busy in helping with the evacuation of a large hospital, and on the last day of evacuation supplied 100 cars to supplement the buses in taking children to their billets. The branch also fed between 2,000 and 3,000 children each day during evacuation.

Devon women were said to be co-operating wholeheartedly with the work of the Women's Voluntary Service for Civil Defence. By the beginning of December, centres had been opened in all areas of the county and the women were particularly busy with the evacuation in the south and east of Devon.

On the morning of Sunday 3 December, four convicts tried to escape from Dartmoor Prison. Two were caught before they could leave their cells but the other two, Reginald Mead and Albert Beard, got away. They scaled the outer wall using ropes and boards and made off across the prison gardens early in the morning. Fifty prison warders

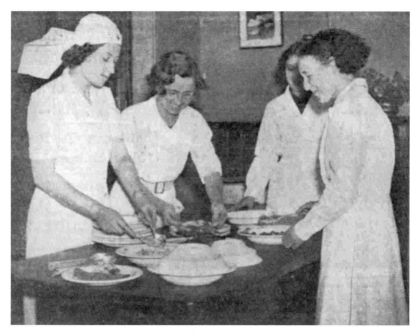

After the children were evacuated from the Devon and Cornwall Female Orphanage, it was used as a hostel for war nurses. They are pictured serving the midday meal.

Evacuated children of the Devon and Cornwall Female Orphanage enjoy a meal at their new home at Arlington House, Teignmouth.

Nurses at the Devon and Cornwall Female Orphanage busy at a sewing machine.

Returning home from duty, war nurses in Plymouth eagerly search for their letters and parcels at the hostel.

and fifty policemen searched the moors in heavy rain. The escapees were wet through and barefoot when they gave themselves up at a farm about eight miles from the prison. Mr J.A. Reep, of Nattor Farm, said that the two convicts had come to his door and asked his housekeeper for something to drink. Edward Maunder, a builder and decorator from Mary Tavy, who was doing some work on the farm, at once recognised

Members of the Women's Land Army helping out on a farm in Devon during November 1939.

the men from the description issued. He questioned them and they admitted being the escaped convicts and said that they wanted to give themselves up.

Maunder said, 'They asked me to ring up the police to take them back to prison as soon as possible. They had only the remains of socks on their feet and were wet through. Mead was absolutely worn out. Beard seemed to be made of harder stuff but he too had had enough of it. While waiting for the police to arrive, we gave the two men a hot meal and drinks and dry clothes and generally made them as comfortable as possible.'

On 13 December, the first major naval conflict took place which would later become known as the Battle of the River Plate. The German battleship, *Graf Spee* was sighted in the South Atlantic by an Allied cruiser squadron comprising HMS *Exeter*, HMS *Ajax* and the New Zealand light cruiser, *Achilles*. *Graf Spee* had been disrupting and raiding merchant ships when she was engaged by the smaller ships of the Allied force. Although the *Exeter* was heavily pounded by the German battleship, they refused to let their prey escape. Many were killed on board the *Exeter* and most of her guns were knocked out of action. However, the *Graf Spee* was forced to retreat and headed towards Montevideo for cover. A huge naval force waited for the *Graf Spee*'s return. However, Hitler ordered the ship to be scuttled off the coast of Uruguay on 17 December.

On 18 December, King George VI visited Plymouth. The visit was kept very quiet with many in Plymouth not knowing his arrival. He spoke to officers and men at Millbay Docks and later inspected the ranks of the Royal Naval Barracks. This was followed by brief tours of the Royal William Victualling Yard and the Royal Naval Engineering College at Manadon. Afterwards, he had an evening meal at Hamoaze House before leaving the city.

War nurses in Plymouth catching up with the latest reports in the newspapers.

Recruits to the Royal Armoured Corps receiving instruction on the working of an internal combustion engine.

HMS Exeter *was heavily pounded by the German battleship,* Graf Spee, *but they refused to let their prey escape. The* Graf Spee *was forced to retreat and headed towards Montevideo for cover where it was later scuttled on Hitler's orders.*

The marriage of Mr Arthur John Wibberley and his bride, Miss Olivia McCandliss, at Buckland Monachorum Church during December 1939. The bridegroom was the son of the late Mr J. Wibberley, a former Plymouth city engineer.

The *Express and Echo* during December reported on a death due to the lighting restrictions. Mr George Pearce, aged 68, of 51 Newport Road, Barnstaple, died in the North Devon Infirmary on the previous Monday, from injuries received in a black-out accident in Litchdon Street, Barnstaple, during the weekend. The coroner pointed out that this unfortunate accident was the first of its kind in the town since the lighting restrictions were brought into force.

All over Devon, there were plans to make Christmas for evacuees from London as good as possible. Mrs H. Corson, of the WVS in Kingsbridge, stated, 'I have two evacuees, each aged 14, and two daughters of my own and I mean to see that they have the best Christmas possible in spite of the war. We are all going into Plymouth for a shopping expedition before Christmas. Then on Christmas Day, we shall have a big family party – foster family, too, of course – and later that week, we shall go to Torquay to the cinema.'

Christmas parties with presents were arranged at Kingsbridge for the children as well as other entertainment. All over the region, as well as Christmas treats, groups of children were taken to the cinema and to see the yearly pantomime, 'Aladdin'.

Lady Astor pictured with evacuees at Plymouth's main railway station. Many children were evacuated to Devon to stay with relatives and family friends. Many saw it as an adventure but others were upset to be leaving their parents behind.

On the approach to Christmas, the *Express and Echo* reported that despite the difficult times, the Christmas season at Exeter would not be without a Nativity play. Members of the University College of the South West and some friends from the city planned to perform at St David's Church on 18 and 19 December. Although the black-out had made the presentation of such plays difficult the problem had been overcome by lighting the stage by candles. It was hoped that, through local effort, one of the traditional events of Christmas would be rewarded by generous contributions to the cause on behalf of which it was being held. Admission to the play was free but there was to be a silver collection.

The *Western Morning News* of Friday 29 December carried information about the forthcoming New Year's celebrations. Some of the familiar features which marked the arrival of the New Year in the past would be absent in Plymouth on the eve of 1940. Owing to the black-out and other war time conditions and restrictions, the committee responsible for organising the midnight service in the Guildhall Square had abandoned it for this year. Silence was also to reign in Sutton Harbour, where there were usually a considerable number of East Coast steam drifters in the port for herring fishing. It had been their practice to welcome the New Year with a barrage of sound from their sirens, hooters and whistles, but, however, none of the boats were in the harbour this year. Even if there were any, their customary concatenation would be forbidden under the Control of Noises (Defence) Order.

Inquiries by the *Western Morning News* among hotels and cafes did not indicate that the number of parties over the week-end would be above the normal, and those that have been arranged would take place on Monday. One of those was the New Year celebration of the Caledonian Society at the Continental Hotel. Applications for tickets for the supper and dance had been numerous and the Scottish custom of playing in the haggis to the music of the bagpipe was to be observed. The Duke of Cornwall Hotel also announced a New Year's Day dinner and dance.

CHAPTER 2

1940 – The Battle of Britain

On 1 January, two million men aged between 19 and 27 were called up for military service in Great Britain.

Sugar, bacon and butter were all rationed on 8 January. Other essentials such as meat, tea, biscuits, jam, cheese, eggs, lard, milk and breakfast cereals as well as canned and dried fruit were subsequently also rationed. Before the war, 55 million tons of food was imported into Britain from other countries. After 1939, the government had to restrict the amount of food coming into the country because the British supply ships were being attacked by German submarines. Rationing of food lasted until July 1954.

Over 11,000 ration books were issued by the Sidmouth food office alone. It was stated that vegetarians and Jews would not receive an additional allowance because they did not eat bacon and ham.

At Tavistock gas indicator boards were set up in case there was a mustard gas attack. The presence of the gas caused red spots to appear on the indicator boards. Fortunately, they were never called into use.

On 16 January the oil tanker *Inverdargle* hit a mine while off Foreland Point near Lynmouth. The ensuing fire could be seen from the North Devon coast. Lifeboats from Minehead, Ilfracombe and Lynmouth went to the vessel's aid. Altogether forty-two crew members of the tanker lost their lives.

On 17 January a spell of freezing weather hit the country causing the River Thames to freeze.

On Thursday 18 January the *Western Morning News* reported that the Admiralty had issued a list of officers and men missing from three submarines including *Seahorse*, *Undine*, and *Starfish*. It said that a deep shadow has been cast over many a West Country home.

Of the ships' company of 108 who, in the words of the Prime Minister, were engaged 'on particularly hazardous service,' which led to the loss of the submarines, over twenty officers and ratings were West Countrymen or had definite associations with the West, and many others were from the Devonport Division.

It was suggested that some of those reported missing could be prisoners of war in Germany, for, as the Admiralty communiqué stated, the German wireless had announced that part of the crews of the *Undine* and *Starfish* had been rescued, but their names were not available.

On 30 January HMS *Ajax* arrived back at Devonport after its skirmish with the German battleship *Graf Spee* in the South Atlantic. Huge crowds gathered to welcome the ship to Plymouth. The warship had been damaged in the fight and had also suffered casualties.

Children who had been evacuated from London to Devon were visited by their parents during January. Special excursions were run by the Southern Railway so that the reunion could take place.

QUALITY TELLS!

DIG FOR VICTORY

We have everything you want, all BRITISH made, at competitive prices.

SPADES, FORKS, TROWELS, ROLLERS, RAKES, HOES, NETTING, TRELLIS.

NOW IS THE TIME TO GET YOUR LAWN MOWER OVERHAULED !

DEVON & SOMERSET STORES Ltd.

EXETER & TAUNTON

Phone 3206 EXETER.
Phone 2208 TAUNTON.

If you buy it at the Stores IT'S GOOD !

An advert in the Express and Echo of Monday 22 January for Devon and Somerset Stores Ltd who provided all the tools needed to 'Dig for Victory'.

Digging for Victory on Plymouth Hoe. With food shortages, many of Plymouth's city parks were turned into allotments. Here the crop is potatoes. Vegetables were not rationed but were often in short supply. People who had gardens were encouraged to plant vegetables instead of flowers.

Winter chill

The winter weather in Devon was particularly cold and many household pipes froze. The story of the cold weather was told in the *Western Morning News* of 30 January. It stated that housewives in mid-Devon who cracked eggs for cooking purposes found them frozen solid. One of the hardest hit communities was Drewsteignton where water supplies were cut off and for a time the electricity supply failed. From other areas came reports of rivers freezing over for the first time in many years and dislocation of transport services.

Villages were isolated and whole streets in towns were deprived of water for days on end. Road traffic came to an almost complete standstill and hundreds of miles of roads were partially paralysed in mid-Devon. Beer and mineral water bottles exploded due to their crystallized contents and village pumps which had been used for hundreds of years split open.

For days the only means of communication with the residents of Drewsteignton was through use of the telephone. One inhabitant told the *Western Morning News*: 'It is unbelievably cold here and you can imagine what it's like without water and lighting and no means of getting anywhere.'

Other small towns on Dartmoor couldn't be reached by road and it was reported that the Torbay area was approaching a water famine during the week of the remarkably severe weather. This wasn't due to a shortage but was because tanks and pipes had become frozen in hundreds of houses. Some people had had burst pipes twice in one week and some woke in the morning to find that they could skate on the floors of their dining rooms and bathrooms. Icicles were hanging from ceilings.

Ice covering the River Taw at Barnstaple, on each side of the Long Bridge, thickened to such an extent that many people ventured on the frozen surface and walked safely across the river. In the Okehampton district, in some places, there were drifts of snow several feet deep. An unparalleled event was the freezing over of the Kingsbridge Estuary, while for the first time for twenty years the whole of Slapton Ley was a solid sheet of ice, on which skating and sliding were enjoyed. The Dartmouth district experienced one of the coldest periods within living memory and on one morning, the boat float was found to be frozen over. At Hatherleigh, the weather in one week was the worst for a quarter of a century and the River Lew was frozen over for the first time since 1916.

The East Devon area had its full share of the intensely cold weather. A thin film of ice covered Exmouth Dock with the ice being about a quarter of an inch thick. At Sidmouth, the weather was the coldest in twenty-five years and for five days skating was in full swing on the frozen Sid Abbey pond. For the first time in living memory, fishermen returned to the East Devon shore in their drifters after many hours' herring fishing in the bay, to find the sides and bottoms of their boats coated with ice.

By 1940 agriculture had lost 30,000 men to the British Army and another 15,000 to other vital work. The severe shortage of labour prompted the government to form the Land Army. By 1944 there were over 80,000 women working on the land doing anything from milking and general farm work to cutting down trees and working in saw mills.

The Agriculture Committee realised the devastation caused by rabbits and urged farmers to shoot them. Rabbit was in demand and was much sought after by housewives, as well as chefs and hotels, who were all living with rationing.

Farms which kept over fifty hens had to send all their eggs to the Ministry. For this reason, many farmers ensured that they only had forty-nine.

On 15 February, HMS *Exeter* returned to Devonport. It had suffered extensive damage and had previously called into the Falkland Islands for temporary repairs. The vessel was fitted with false gun turrets at the front so as to fool the enemy. Sixty of the ship's crew had lost their lives and had been buried in the South Atlantic.

The *Western Morning News* carried a report about the ship's homecoming on Friday 16 February. It read:

HMS *Exeter*, name-ship of Devon's 'ever faithful' city is home. In the grey dawn of yesterday, the cruiser slipped from her escort and dropped her anchor in Plymouth Sound. It was the end of one of the most glorious chapters in the present war history of the Royal Navy. After her epic part in the Battle of the River Plate, when, in company with the cruisers *Ajax* and *Achilles* , she rid the seas of the German raiding pocket-battleship *Graf Spee*, she limped southwards

Land Army girls marching past the City Museum in Plymouth. By 1940, agriculture had lost 30,000 men to the British Army and another 15,000 to other vital work. The severe shortage of labour prompted the government to form the Land Army. By 1944, there were over 80,000 women working on the land doing anything from milking and general farm work to cutting down trees and working in saw mills.

to the security of the Falkland Islands. There she licked her wounds of almost mortal severity, once more took to the open sea, and yesterday she reached home waters, there to be given a reception in keeping with the gallantry of her crew. It was a proud day for the West Country, and the occasion was made the most auspicious by the fact that the First Lord of the Admiralty (Mr Winston Churchill), the Chancellor of the Exchequer (Sir John Simon) and the First Sea Lord (Admiral Sir Dudley Pound) made a special journey from London to welcome the *Exeter* on behalf of the nation.

No sooner had the cruiser dropped anchor than the following message from the Lords of the Admiralty was received: 'Their lordships welcome the *Exeter* back to her home port and congratulate you all on bringing your ship safely home, in spite of the damage received during the Battle of the River Plate, in which you upheld the best fighting traditions of the Navy. We hope you will soon enjoy well-earned leave.'

The day after the *Exeter* arrived in Plymouth, its crew marched through the streets of the city to the Guildhall for a civic luncheon.

On 23 February, the king decorated the heroes of HMS *Exeter* and *Ajax*. They received a terrific reception in London and there was an historic march through the city.

The *Western Morning News* of 29 February carried a story about two sailors who had been found on a raft. The vicar of St Andrew's Church in Plymouth referred to Denmark as a 'gallant and friendly nation' as he conducted the funeral service of the two Danish sailors, Herluf Christian Wilhem Bidstrup and Carlo Petersen, who had been found on a raft by a British warship. Petersen was dead when rescued and Bidstrup died a few hours later in hospital. 'We are here today,' said Mr Martin, 'to do honour to two men who, after a week of most intense suffering and deprivation, have passed over to the other side. These men belonged to a gallant and friendly nation, which, though neutral as far as the war is concerned, is facing hardship and cruel sufferings and even death as a result of unwarrantable piracy on the deep seas. Our sincerest sympathy goes out to the families who have been thus bereaved. We join in praying that the day may soon come when aggression shall cease and peace be established, for in that day the seas shall be free to all nations, so that each may go about their lawful business unhampered and unafraid.'

Before the coffins were borne from the church by sailors of the warship which rescued the dead men, the Danish National Anthem and the Last Post were played on the organ by Dr Harry Moreton. When the bodies were conveyed from the mortuary in Vauxhall Street to St Andrew's Church, all traffic in Old Town Street was stopped. The funeral cortege was composed of two cars containing the coffins, each of which was draped with the Danish flag, accompanied by a detachment of sailors from the warship.

The *Western Times* of Friday 1 March carried a story under the headline PLATE BATTLE ENSIGN PRESENTED TO EXETER. It read:

Men who helped to send the Nazi pocket-battleship *Graf Spee* to her ignominious end in the River Plate battle came to Exeter yesterday. They were the officers and ratings of HMS *Exeter*, the city's name-ship. Citizens, thrilled by their exploit in the Southern Atlantic, let themselves go with unprecedented enthusiasm. Fifty thousand people, cheering wildly, lined the route along which these gallant sea dogs marched from St David's station to the Guildhall. The city proudly did them honour. During this memorable visit there was an official lunch, the freedom of the city was conferred upon Captain F.S. Bell CB, commanding officer of the *Exeter*, and this noble leader among men handed to the mayor the ship's ensign as a memento of an historic sea action.

On 11 March, meat rationing was introduced.

The *Western Times* of Thursday 21 March featured a story about a 15-year-old bugler of the Plymouth Division of the Royal Marines who on the previous Sunday had been presented with a gold half-hunter watch in recognition of his gallant bearing when his ship was torpedoed and sunk. Bugler R.D. Emmerson, of 43, Briar Road, Compton, was the youngest of the ship's company of HMS *Courageous*. Residents at Compton, who had known him since he was a schoolboy, were so impressed by his bearing during and since the action that they made a collection. With it, the watch was purchased and presented to him at a special parade at the RM Barracks. It was stated that Emmerson was just going on duty when his ship was hit. As it heeled over, he asked an officer what he should do, and was told, 'jump for it.' Before he did so, he lashed his bugle to the side of the ship. He was in the water for 40 minutes before being picked up.

Farm workers picking daffodils at Tamerton Creek near Plymouth during April. The flowers were destined for the London market.

On 31 March, Oswald Mosley and thirty-three fascist sympathisers were interned.

On 1 April, Number 10 Royal Australian Air Force Squadron replaced 204 Squadron who had left for North Africa. They stayed in Plymouth for the duration of the war and left in October 1945.

In the spring of 1940, notification was received that more evacuees were heading for the county. Ilfracombe welcomed 200 children from the Dagenham area while Barnstaple expected 2,500 evacuees to be billeted in the town.

The *Western Morning News* of Saturday 6 April reported that housewives were hoarding farthings. Apparently farthings were worrying the Ministry of Food. In fact, the ministry was so concerned that it circulated a letter to all food offices about the small coin. It mentioned that people were hoarding farthings, or putting them aside as they did not want to be bothered with them. Under the present system of rationing, the little coin was essential for the purchase of small quantities of rationed commodities. West Country food executive officials were asked to take every opportunity of drawing attention to the need for the free circulation of Britain's smallest coin.

On Saturday 13 April an official notification was given that the Paper Controller had reduced the ration of paper from 60 per cent of pre-war consumption to

The public air raid shelters in King's Gardens, Plymouth. Many homes had their own shelters which were erected in their back gardens. These Anderson shelters were made of corrugated iron and were issued free to people earning less than £250 a year. People with higher incomes had to pay £7. They were first issued in 1939 and undoubtedly saved many lives.

30 per cent. So drastic was the curtailment of the raw material that it greatly affected the newspaper industry.

On 23 April, purchase tax and an increased duty on tobacco were introduced as part of the War Budget. Income tax went up and beer was raised by 1d a pint. Whisky, tobacco and postal charges were all raised and it was hoped that the budget would raise £1,234,000,000 towards the estimated expenditure for the year of £2,667,000,000.

The *Express and Echo* of Friday 26 April carried a story under the headline MAYOR OF EXETER'S APPEAL FOR RECRUITS. It read:

'It is of the utmost importance that we should have our civil defence force complete to the last man and woman and equipped to the last button.' Thus the mayor of Exeter (Mr R. Glave Saunders), appealing, during an interval in the programme at the Gaumont Palace, Exeter, last evening, for more recruits for the voluntary services of the city's ARP organisation. The mayor observed that the audience would have gathered from the picture they had seen, the sort of enemy they were fighting, very clever, utterly ruthless and callous, whose word was not worth the paper it was written on.

A deflated barrage balloon lands on the roof of the Swarthmore on Plymouth Hoe on 3 May 1940.

'It was difficult,' he went on, 'to bring home to the people of these islands our immediate danger, not only from air attack by bombs, including high explosive, incendiary, and gas, but from actual invasion.'

On 10 May Neville Chamberlain resigned as Prime Minister. Winston Churchill took his place. Churchill offered Lord Astor the wartime post of Minister of Agriculture but the position was declined because Astor felt that his first duty was to the people of Plymouth.

The *Exeter and Plymouth Gazette* of Friday 10 May carried a story about allotment holders and produce. At a meeting of Exmouth Food Control Committee it was stated that allotment holders would be unable to dispose of their surplus vegetables by retail unless they had been in the habit of doing so before the war. 'Then what is to be done with the surplus?' asked Captain C.P. Shrubb. Mr R.S. Rainford, the Food Executive Officer, said there was no objection to its disposal through wholesalers. The Reverend T.G. Shelmerdine considered it was discouraging after people had been urged to grow as much as possible. They were likely to get a raw deal by selling wholesale. It was agreed to make representations to the Minister of Food asking if they would be allowed to issue licenses to allotment holders enabling them to dispose of any surplus by retail.

Two members of the Civil Defence Force in Plymouth quickly carry a small child to safety during a gas mask drill. The men are well protected with gas masks, overalls and safety boots.

On 14 May recruitment commenced for the Local Defence Volunteers. They would later be renamed the Home Guard.

On 16 May, the internment of aliens living in the country began on a large scale.

The *North Devon Journal* of Thursday 16 May reported on a discussion by Barnstaple's Education Committee about gas masks. The mayor of Barnstaple (Councillor C.F. Dart JP) stated, 'While I am not an alarmist, I think we are nearer using gas masks today than we were eight months ago, and if we can read the writing on the wall, as indicated by the Prime Minister, there are events that may possibly happen.'

At the meeting of Barnstaple Education Committee, the secretary (Mr H.H. Hawkins), reported that a new order in respect to gas masks said that in future damage would have to be made good. The mayor asked, 'Do the children know they are to be made

Gas mask drill for children. All children were issued with gas masks which came in small cardboard boxes. Everyday at school, they would have a gas mask drill. Many children found the drills hard to take seriously and their masks were a source for fun and games.

responsible for damage?' He was told that schools had been informed. His Worship agreed damage through negligence should be made good by those to whom gas masks had been issued but it was a different matter if the rubber was to perish.

Dunkirk and refugees
Between 26 May and 4 June, the evacuation of the British Expeditionary Force at Dunkirk took place. Over 300,000 troops were saved and returned to England. All types of boats, many from Devon, took part in the rescue including fishing vessels, pleasure boats, lifeboats and merchant marine boats. The flotilla of small boats undoubtedly saved thousands of lives. Amongst the paddle steamers involved in the rescue were the *Glen Avon* , which was well-known in Ilfracombe; the *Devon Belle*, a passenger boat on the River Dart; the *Brighton Belle*, which rescued 800 troops, and the *Devonia*, which had to be abandoned at Dunkirk after an enemy attack.

Many returning servicemen recuperated in Devon before rejoining their units.

At the end of May, large numbers of French refugees began arriving in Plymouth fleeing from advancing German forces. After being given food and temporary accommodation, they travelled to Liverpool until arrangements could be made to return them home once the war was over.

The city became incredibly crowded and barracks were full. Over 100 Polish men arrived from France to enlist in the exiled Polish navy and they were billeted at Plymouth before moving to a camp at Westward Ho!

During May and June 1940, Germany invaded France, arriving in Paris on 14 June. By occupying France, they were in a better strategic position to start bombing Great Britain.

Approximately 80,000 French troops arrived at Turnchapel on 2 June having recently been evacuated from Dunkirk. People from all over the city provided accommodation and baths for the men. A canteen service was set up at the docks.

Devon soldiers take a break to play a keenly watched game of draughts.

Members of the BEF recovering from wounds received in Flanders and Northern France. They are seen on the terrace at a hospital near Exeter during June.

On 4 June, Winston Churchill made his famous, 'We will fight them on the beaches' speech in the House of Commons.

On 10 June, Italy declared war on France and Great Britain.

The *Western Morning News* of Wednesday 12 June reported on the round up of Italians in Devon. It stated that following Italy's declaration of war, six Italians from Exeter, twelve from the administrative county of Devon and four from Plymouth had been interned. Police had kept protective watch of an ice-cream shop in Plymouth when a crowd of people demonstrated their resentment towards the proprietor. Women who assembled outside the shop and made hostile remarks were moved along. Some people still went into the shop to buy ice-cream.

There were a number of people of Italian extraction in Plymouth, but the majority of them, although bearing typical Italian names, were naturalized. Some took out papers during the Abyssinian War, while other families had been in the country for generations. Several businesses that had been run by Italians had

A wounded Tommy takes a walk assisted by two nurses.

changed ownership. At one shop, the name was scraped off the door and an inquiry for the proprietor elicited the reply 'He is not here anymore.' One tradesman, whose parents were naturalized forty years previously said that he was in a quandary because he had kept his Italian name. 'I was born in Plymouth,' he said, 'but I'm afraid people won't believe I'm British.'

Mr Lovell Dunstan, the vice-consul, had erased all reference to the Italian Consulate from his business premises in Southside Street. 'It is finished,' he said, and, referring to Italy's declaration of war, he added, 'Italy will have to suffer for it.'

Damage was caused to the front of a cafe in High Street, Exeter, during a demonstration when a small crowd assembled outside the premises. There was some disturbance, during which a large plate-glass window was smashed and three small panes in the door were also damaged. The demonstrators did not enter the cafe and no damage was done inside. The city police were promptly on the scene and made investigation. The cafe was temporarily closed and the window was boarded up pending repair.

On 17 June, RMS *Lancastria* was destroyed by the Luftwaffe with the loss of 4,000 lives while evacuating British troops and nationals from Saint-Nazaire after the Fall of France. However, the people of Devon were not to know about it until long after the war as Winston Churchill had ordered a news blackout on the story during what was regarded as Britain's darkest hour just after Dunkirk. In fact the sinking of the *Lancastria* resulted in the largest loss of life in British maritime history – more than the *Titanic* and *Lusitania* combined and it would not be until the 1970s that the true facts were revealed.

The ex-Great Western Channel Islands ferry *St Helier* moored in Plymouth Sound at 5.30pm on 18 June. It had been diverted while on its way from Southampton to La Pallice in France and when it left it was attacked by two enemy planes. The crew returned heavy fire, hitting both planes and causing a bomb on board one to fall short of its target. After running the gauntlet of an electrical storm and a threatened attack by an enemy submarine, the vessel arrived safely back in Plymouth Sound on 21 June.

A young lady hands out gifts of flowers to French troops as they wait at the quayside to embark during June. The flowers including pinks, carnations and roses were fresh from the Devon countryside.

Above left: Some of the evacuated children from London who were photographed at Plymouth station on Thursday 13 June. They were on their way to Cornwall.

Above right: The evacuated children travelled on 30 special trains. When they arrived at Plymouth, they were given drinks by St John's Ambulance Association members and their helpers.

Right: A spaniel which took part in the retreat from Dunkirk. It was the mascot of the French troops and shared with the men all the grim days during the battles in Flanders and Northern France.

Thousands of French soldiers taken off the beaches at Dunkirk re-embarked during June at a West Country port before their return to France. A service band played on the quayside as they boarded the waiting transports.

Above left: *A French officer buying an emblem from a nurse to help raise money for the British Red Cross Society flag day in Devon during June.*

Above right: *Drinks were provided to the evacuees when they stopped at Plymouth. Many were en route to Cornwall.*

Below: *Child evacuees from London arriving in Exeter during the beginning of June. Almost 3,000 children needed to be accommodated.*

On 18 June, Winston Churchill gave a speech in the House of Commons where he said:

What General Weygand has called the Battle of France is over. The Battle of Britain is about to begin. Upon this battle depends the survival of Christian civilisation. Upon it depends our own British life and the long continuity of our institutions and our Empire. The whole fury and might of the enemy must very soon be turned on us. Hitler knows that he will have to break us in this island or lose the war. If we can stand up to him, all Europe may be free and the life of the world may move forward into broad, sunlit uplands. But if we fail, then the whole world, including the United States, including all that we have known and cared for, will sink into the abyss of a new Dark Age made more sinister, and perhaps more protracted, by the lights of a perverted science. Let us therefore brace ourselves to our duties, and so bear ourselves that, if the British Empire and its Commonwealth last for a thousand years, men will still say, 'This was their finest hour.'

The *Western Morning News* of Thursday 27 June included a story about the government's decision not to make Plymouth an evacuation area. When Plymouth's Emergency Committee met, the town clerk, Mr Colin Campbell, reported that arising out of representations made to the Ministry of Health by the committee, that Plymouth should now be regarded as an evacuation area, the ministry indicated that the whole position relating to evacuation was under constant review by the government.

They stated that they would not hesitate to make such changes to the present plans as might from time to time become necessary, but it was not at present proposed to declare Plymouth an evacuation area.

The committee decided to suspend granting holidays to the professional, technical, and clerical staffs of the corporation until they had an opportunity of giving further consideration to the question at their meeting next week, when there was to be presented reports from the various departments of the corporation as to the expediency of granting holidays.

Further sites for communal air-raid shelters in different parts of the city were approved. Tenders were accepted for the provision of gates, locks and keys, for such shelters. An offer was received from the Beechwood factory, Alexandra Road and Finewell Street, for the use of their air-raid shelters for the general public outside business hours.

On 30 June, the German forces occupied the Channel Islands. The British Government had decided that the islands had no strategic importance and would not be defended. Many of the islands' children were evacuated to mainland Britain. The Channel Islands were liberated on 9 May 1945.

There was a worry that enemy seaplanes could land on the rivers Tamar, Lynher and Plym and the owners of small boats were asked to create a barrier by positioning their boats in such a way to prevent enemy planes landing.

Plymouth's first alert was on 30 June 1940. When the siren sounded, most made their way to the air-raid shelters. The alert lasted an hour but there were no incidents.

The bombing of Plymouth
The first bombs fell on Plymouth on 6 July 1940. They were dropped shortly before noon on eight houses at Swilly Road, Devonport. A man, a woman and a boy were killed and six people were injured. Plymouth had 602 alerts altogether and 59 raids in which bombs were dropped. The last bombs fell on 30 April 1944.

Meanwhile, also on 6 July, two high explosive bombs were dropped at Galmpton near Brixham. There were two casualties although little damage to property. A huge crater was left.

On 7 July 1940, Plymouth suffered its second serious attack. A German bomber flew low over the east end of the city towards Laira. The plane was so low that a man working at the gasworks opened fire on it with a shotgun. The gasworks were the target but the stick of bombs fell on South Milton Street and Home Sweet Home Terrace. A policeman and a soldier on duty in the area were killed by the blasts together with five other people.

On 8 July 1940 Plymouth had its third serious raid in the early morning. Four bombs were dropped on Devonport in the vicinity of Marlborough Street and Morice Square. A local butcher, Mr Slee, was killed when his shop took a direct hit. Three other people were seriously injured and another seven had less serious injuries. Three of the bombs fell near to the Royal Albert Hospital but there was little damage.

On 10 July the Battle of Britain began. Germany's plan was to force Britain into a negotiated peace with an air and sea blockade. Major ports were bombed by the Germans and the order was issued for the Luftwaffe to achieve superiority in the air over the RAF by bombing airfields and the infrastructure surrounding them. As the battle progressed, factories involved in aircraft production were also attacked. The RAF prevented the Luftwaffe from gaining air superiority which forced Hitler to

A man rescues his dog from the wreckage of destroyed homes.

cancel a proposed invasion of the United Kingdom, codenamed Operation Sea Lion. The battle proved crucial to the security of Great Britain.

Also on 10 July 1940, bombs dropped on Exeter Street and the Hoe district in Plymouth killing five people and injuring seven. Three people were killed near the Hoe where there was damage to large residential properties at Leigham Terrace and Carlisle Avenue. Civilians felt more terror as they were machine gunned by planes as they ran for the shelters. Luckily, no-one was hit.

In Plymouth, during summer, an anti-gossip and will-to-win campaign was launched. It was felt that careless talk could lead to the movements of units and their activities being discovered by the enemy.

The *Western Morning News* of Saturday 20 July reported that a Nazi plane had machine gunned a street in Devon. The story read:

Machine guns spluttering furiously, a twin-engined bomber dived out of the clouds over a south-western town yesterday evening. Bullets bespattered the streets. After quick bursts across the streets, the Nazi plane banked sharply over the residential part of a nearby village. There, the Germans released eight bombs in rapid succession. One fell in a school yard. The school buildings were wrecked by the blast of the explosion and fragments of bombs, but the buildings were empty. Another bomb fell in an adjoining garden, churning up masses of earth as it carved a crater. The other six fell in neighbouring fields. No one was killed or even injured. The plane had a warm reception from anti-aircraft fire, and it soon moved towards the coast. British fighters rapidly appeared and swept out to sea in its wake. It is believed that the German raider was punctured by an anti-aircraft shell, which burst close on its tail just after the bombs had been released. The plane was losing height when it moved off, and it is assumed that it came down at sea.

On 21 July 1940, North Road Station in Plymouth was the target during a series of five raids. It was completely missed but bombs hit York Place and did extensive damage and also killed an elderly woman and a young boy. Another bomb hit the premises of Edmund Walker, a ball-bearing specialist, in Albany Ope and extensive damage nearby made many families homeless.

The *Western Morning News* of Wednesday 31 July carried the story of an entertainer, performing at the Alhambra Theatre in Devonport, who had previously appeared in front of Hitler. Mr Murray Walters, a 32-year-old Australian vaudeville star, was believed to be the last Briton to leave Germany after war was declared, Walters was appearing in the Berlin Wintergarten when war was declared. He told a *Western Morning News* reporter that he had given a special performance for Hitler in the Wintergarten. 'I was at times no more than about ten feet away from the Fuhrer,' he said, 'and as I look back now I wonder why I did not shoot him with the gun I use in my act. The guns I am using now are, of course, harmless, apart from my rifle, and that has only a very small range, but the guns I was using in Germany were the real thing. It is a wonder to me that I was allowed to get as close to him as I did.'

Mr Walters had been appearing in Plymouth and Devonport for fifteen years. During his last visit to the Palace Theatre, Plymouth, he jumped into the water off Stonehouse Bridge with his hands secured.

Fears of German parachutists landing on Dartmoor led to a watch being set up by farmers, the Home Guard and members of the hunt. Women rode with the patrols, carrying binoculars.

On 9 August, Birmingham was badly bombed.

The *Western Morning News* of Wednesday 14 August carried the story of mistaken identity. Church bells rang out in three villages in south-west England on the previous night. However, it proved to be a false alarm. A pilot had bailed out from a British plane, and a well meaning but misguided spectator thought that the invasion had started and dashed to the parish church and rang the bells. The rumour travelled quickly and soon the bells were ringing in two neighbouring villages. Calm was restored when members of the Home Guard went round and explained the real facts.

The first raid on Exeter took place on 20 August when a single plane dropped bombs in the St Thomas area. Slight damage was caused to property. Brixham was also bombed during August which was followed by a raid on Torquay two hours later. Eight bombs exploded in Torquay which damaged property and caused slight injuries to residents. Newton Abbot railway station came under attack and high explosive bombs were dropped. The area was sprayed with German machine-gun fire. There was considerable damage and fourteen people lost their lives.

In Parliament on 20 August, Winston Churchill paid tribute to the RAF when he said, 'Never in the field of human conflict was so much owed by so many to so few.'

A Nazi bomber was shot down in the South West and the story was carried by the *Western Morning News* on Friday 23 August:

Trading stopped in a market town in the south-west when the drone of aeroplane engines was heard, followed by rapid bursts of machine gun fire. Looking up, the people saw a German bomber, its swastikas easily discernible, streaking across the sky with a British fighter hot on its tail. Rapidly the machines disappeared over the hills, before they passed out of sight when black smoke began to pour from the German machine. Later it was learnt that the German had crashed in a lonely part of the area some twelve miles away. The plane burst into flames, which were visible for many miles around. The local fire brigade was called into action. The bomber had crashed on a farm where an eye witness, Mr T. Clemens, stated that he was raking and loading corn when he saw a plane coming straight towards him. It was losing height and it dropped before it reached him. Great clouds of smoke arose just afterwards. Leaving the cornfield he went in the direction of the smoke and saw three men belonging to the plane in the charge of the police and the Home Guard. The fourth occupant of the enemy plane was dead. Apparently he had fallen from it before it reached the earth. The men were armed with revolvers but they gave them up. Their faces were scorched and blackened. The first remark made by one of the Germans was, 'Is this Britain?'

Animals were also evacuated to Devon. Here, Horace, a baby elephant, arrived at Paignton from Chessington, Surrey in August. He was accompanied by other animals and was on view to the public at Primley Zoo (later Paignton Zoo) towards the end of the month.

More air raids

On 24 August the first air raid took place on London. In retaliation the RAF bombed Berlin for the first time on 25/26 August.

On 27 August 1940, Plymouth had its longest alert so far during the night with relays of German planes heading north. Bombs were dropped over a scattered area including Millbay, Crownhill and Ford. The worst incident was when a bomb dropped on Ford House, the Public Assistance Institution. Thirteen people were killed and many others injured. One young boy was saved when a nurse shielded him with her body. She was knocked unconscious but later recovered.

The following day, 28 August 1940, six bombs and several incendiaries were dropped in the countryside between St Budeaux and Crownhill in Plymouth. Incendiaries which threatened the woodlands were quickly dealt with by the Auxiliary Fire Service while the bombs fell away from houses and did no serious damage.

There was an expectation during September that German forces would try to land in Devon and there were many false alarms. The Home Guard erected barbed-wire barriers across the road in the northern district of Plymouth in anticipation of an invasion.

The *Western Times* of Friday 6 September carried a story about a man who failed to produce his identity card. Arthur William Lugg of Bideford, was sentenced to a fortnight's imprisonment imposed by Bideford Borough Magistrates for failing to produce, when required by a constable, his national registration card and also for failing to produce the card within two days at Bideford Police station. After outlining the facts of the case, Inspector Rendell said that Lugg had made a series of allegations saying the card had been stolen from him. The defendant was told he had had ample time to obtain an identity card and the facts would be reported.

On 7 September, the blitz of London began. It lasted for fifty-seven consecutive nights.

On Monday 9 September, the *Western Morning News* carried the story of a 2am call to the Home Guard over false invasion rumours. The ringing of church bells and amplified voices shattered the still of the black-out, and hammerings on doors were among the incidents that aroused the West Country from its sleep in the early hours of the previous morning. Members of the Home Guard rose from their beds to intercept all traffic. Rumours of the threatened invasion ran rapidly through town and village. These alternated with stories that German agents had been dropped by parachute in remote moorland areas. But with the dawn the true facts slowly filtered through and the Home Guard units were later disbanded. The *Western Morning News* learned that the panic had been a false alarm but it provided a searching practical test of the measures taken to preserve the West Country from attack.

A raid on 11 September resulted in the deaths of thirteen people at the junction of Chapel Street and Emma Place in Stonehouse, Plymouth. Another fifteen were injured, all by a single bomb.

On 13 September the Home Guard manned barricades at Ilfracombe as rumours of German spies spread. ID cards were checked but nothing untoward was discovered.

On 15 September the RAF claimed victory over the Luftwaffe during the Battle of Britain.

On 17 September child evacuees heading for Canada were amongst 245 killed while on board the SS *City of Benares* which was torpedoed and sunk by German submarine *U-48*. Only thirteen of the ninety children survived – six of them after spending a week in an open boat.

The French cutter *Le Part Bleu* arrived at Plymouth during the third week of September. On board were three German agents whose mission involved sabotage. On their return to Germany they presented Hitler with a detailed map showing the location of 48th Division in Devon and gaps in the fortifications on the coast.

On 23 September, King George VI announced the creation of the George Cross.

Plymouth had one of its heaviest daylight attacks on 25 September. Houses in Goschen Street were destroyed by bombs meant for the dockyard at Keyham. There were numerous dogfights during the day between German raiders and British planes. Shells were bursting everywhere proving to be the most spectacular daylight combat that the city had seen. People came out into the street to watch and the heavy barrage made many of the raiders flee, dropping their bombs aimlessly in the Sound.

The *Western Times* of Friday 27 September told of an elderly woman's recent adventure:

To Hitler, a south-west nonagenarian owes two adventures. Her house was one of those on which the Nazi leader's airmen dropped their bombs on a recent occasion. It was necessary for the householder to be removed from the wreckage

German plane wreckage being examined. Little remained of the machine or its crew.

to a new home, and for this purpose a motor car was used. And that was the old lady's first motor car ride.

On 25 September 1940 there was a day of alerts with bombs dropped at Higher St Budeaux and near to Higher Ernesettle Farm in Plymouth. Luckily, there were no casualties. Another bomb was dropped on Agaton Fort, wounding two soldiers. On the same day, bombs fell on Prison Hill at Mutley and homes at Goschen Street, Keyham where five houses were destroyed and several others damaged.

During October, the first George Cross was awarded to Lieutenant R. Davies, a Plymouth man who was the officer in charge of the squad responsible for recovering the St Paul's Cathedral bomb. The notification of the award was published in the *London Gazette* on 1 October. The official announcement stated:

So conscious was Lieutenant Davies of the imminent danger to the Cathedral that, regardless of personal risk, he spared neither himself nor his men in their efforts to locate the bomb. After unremitting effort, during which all ranks knew that an explosion might occur at any moment, the bomb was successfully extricated.

In order to shield his men from further danger, Lieutenant Davies drove away, on his own, the vehicle in which the bomb was removed and personally carried out its disposal.

Above left: Ellen Vardon, aged 11, hailed from sunny Jersey. She said that she was pleased to come to Devon from St Helier before the Nazis arrived in the islands.

Above right: John Pratt, aged 10, was a shy evacuee from London and said that he loved the countryside around Tavistock. He remembered what his mother told him and always carried a gas mask.

Left: Joyce Warwick, aged 12, left her home in London with her mother at the beginning of October. The house next door to them had been bombed.

The *Western Morning News* of Tuesday 22 October reported that someone was handing out white feathers in Plymouth:

The white feather is stalking the streets of Plymouth. A girl is distributing these nauseous emblems. She presented one during the weekend to Mr E.S. Brookes, a journalist attached to a national newspaper. 'At first I felt a surge of resentment,' Mr Brookes, said. 'Then I thought she was probably the kind of unfortunate female who has to live alone with a parrot. So, I said, "Send the rest of the chicken around tomorrow," and walked away. Mr Brookes served in the navy in the Great War, he is now waiting to rejoin the service. He was aboard one of the ships that took part in the bombardment of Cherbourg recently.

The Battle of Britain ended on 31 October.

On Wednesday 6 November, the *Western Morning News* reported that food orders had been breached. A letter was sent to retailers in Plymouth and Devonport pannier markets, calling to their attention the breaches of the Ministry of Food regulations. The Plymouth Food Control Committee stated that a number of cases had been brought to their attention. It was proposed to send retailers dealing in pork, letters regarding the over charging of their products. It was feared that there would always be trouble in the pannier markets because of the unorganised method of trading. The committee said that people came in with produce from their own farms and sold it to procure what was described as 'some pocket money for the end of the week'.

On 6 November bombs fell on Gifford Terrace and Trelawney Road in Plymouth killing four people. On 18 November, a further nine people were killed in an attack at Lipson Vale in the city.

Between 14 and 15 November, Coventry was heavily bombed by the Luftwaffe destroying the centre of the city. On 19 November heavy bombing raids took place on Birmingham, West Bromwich, Dudley and Tipton. Southampton was heavily bombed

Two boys survey the damage after a raid on Plymouth in November 1940. Smoke can be seen billowing out from the oil tanks at Turnchapel.

on 23 November and Bristol was hit the following night. The heavy raids on Bristol resulted in many people being evacuated to Devon.

The *Western Morning News* of Tuesday 26 November carried a story about the true facts about raids on the South West:

'It is no use going to Tavistock, it has been wiped out by the raids,' a resident of South Wales was assured when proposing to visit relatives in Devon. The true facts of Tavistock's raids are that although many alerts have been given, no damage and no casualties have resulted in the urban area. A certain number of bombs have dropped in the rural district, but the damage has been slight and few casualties have resulted. Similar information comes from the Okehampton rural area, whereas the town itself has had only one raid in which bombs have been dropped.'

On 28 November 1940, about 7.30pm, an enemy aircraft dropped four flares over the Mount Batten and Turnchapel areas of Plymouth. Almost straight away one of the hangars at RAF Mount Batten was hit by a high explosive bomb. There was another direct hit on the Admiralty Oil Fuel Depot opposite Turnchapel station. The fierce fire

The first two women trainees at the ministry of munitions training centre in Exeter. They were Mrs M. Austin, who formerly ran a nursing home, and Mrs M. Cobbledick, a housewife. Both volunteered to 'do their bit' for their country. It was stated that half a million women were required to carry out munition work.

Two London evacuees help with gathering cider apples near Holbeton.

that followed so illuminated the sky that people on the Barbican and the Hoe could easily read their newspapers. The fires lasted for five days.

Oreston in Plymouth was also bombed along with Turnchapel, Plymstock, the Cattewater and the Barbican. Ten people were killed at Oreston and four houses were destroyed.

Parcels for the Troops

The *North Devon Journal* of Thursday 12 December carried a story under the headline GREAT WORK FOR TROOPS. It stated that there was no busier place in Barnstaple or North Devon than the Mayoress of Barnstaple's Central Depot for Forces Comforts on the Strand. It was there that 1,500 parcels, one for every Barumite serving in the forces and prisoners of war, were being packed and dispatched. Each parcel was valued at from six shillings to nine shillings and contained a woollen comfort, a pullover, socks, helmet, scarf or mittens, writing pad, biscuits, games, envelopes, cigarettes, sweets and chocolates, soap, shaving kit and face cloth. Each parcel also contained the following Christmas greeting card:

The Mayor, Aldermen, and Burgesses of the borough of Barnstaple send you hearty greetings for Xmas and the sincere hope that the New Year may bring

A family sitting amongst the ruins of their house in Oreston after an attack in November 1940.

peace to all nations. They wish to thank you for the service which you are rendering to bring this war to a successful conclusion.

Charles F. Dart, Mayor, The Guildhall, Barnstaple, Xmas 1940.

Between 12 and 15 December, Sheffield came under attack by the Luftwaffe and 660 were killed. Liverpool was heavily bombed between 20 and 21 December with Manchester being blitzed the following night.

It was reported during December that following an air raid in a South West town, Bertram Arden went to inspect the damage and found part of a heavy bomb. He took it away with him, intending to keep it as a souvenir.

Arden was summoned for removing the article without permission and a police officer stated that owing to the defendant's actions, members of the police force were put to unnecessary trouble. Only after extensive enquiries and a threat that an application would be made for a search warrant, did the defendant admit taking away the bomb part as a souvenir. The police constable who made the investigation said, in cross examination, that Arden was very obstructive. The witness denied using obscene language to the defendant or his mother. Arden was fined £1 and the chairman hoped that the prosecution would be a warning to all not to take away souvenirs.

At the end of the hearing, Arden asked, 'What becomes of the thing now, can I have it?' The Superintendent of Police replied, 'You certainly cannot.'

Supplies of goods in shops were short. However, trading up until Christmas was good as people bought what they could. Leave for the home forces was cancelled over the festive period. Christmas proved to be bomb free with no reported enemy attacks.

The *Western Morning News* of Tuesday 24 December carried a story about a Christmas party in Exeter for evacuees:

Evacuee mothers and children will attend what is probably the largest Christmas party of their lives at the Civic Hall Rest Room, Exeter, tomorrow. About 500 guests are expected, and no effort is being spared to make the programme for them as attractive as possible.

London was heavily bombed on the night of 29 December.

At Tavistock, 400 people sang and danced on New Year's Eve. Many attended church services and hoped for a better year ahead.

On 29 December, Plymouth had its worst raid to date. Bombs fell on the city from the Barbican to Mutley. Eleven people were killed and twelve were seriously injured. Ford House was hit again and its 230 inmates were successfully evacuated.

CHAPTER 3

1941 – The Blitz

There was a lack of church bells to see in the New Year in Devon at the beginning of 1941; ringing them was still forbidden. Many children who had missed their Christmas party attended New Year parties which took place in small villages all over Devon.

New ration books were issued although 3,000 went unclaimed at Plymouth's food offices.

The *Western Morning News* of Wednesday 1 January reported that Devon's care of evacuees was the best. Mr C. Robertson, chairman of the LCC Education Committee, said that 'nowhere throughout the forty counties to which London children had been sent during the present war had evacuation been such an outstanding success as in Devon.'

He was visiting Exmouth to see a section of school children evacuated from London. Mr Robertson also commented, after a visit to Exeter, that whatever the evacuation of parents might have been, the evacuation of unaccompanied school children has been a thorough success, both as regards their health and cultural outlook. At the conclusion of his visit Mr Robertson told a reporter how indebted they were in London to the Devon foster parents for their great kindness to the children and also to the Devon County Education Authorities and the Exeter City Education Committee and the teachers in general for the magnificent way in which they had co-operated in the evacuation scheme.

A government order came into effect in January compelling all businesses to inform fire-fighting services of the arrangements they had made for fire-watching. Fire-watching was made compulsory and all able-bodied citizens between 16 and 60 years of age were invited to assist in the work.

During January owners of premises in Frankfort Street and Russell Street in Plymouth, organised a scheme for fire watching. A committee was appointed to seek the co-operation of occupiers of lock-up shops in the area, either by way of financial aid or personal service. It was estimated that the cost would work out to 10s a week for each shop. All the members of the butchery staff at the Plymouth Co-operative Society including men, women and girls, volunteered for duty in connection with the scheme for the protection of the premises of the company against incendiary

A member of staff from Popham's in Plymouth ready for fire-watching duty.

Members of the Southampton Police Force changed duties with Exeter City Police officers during February. They can be seen here playing billiards after a day's work at Exeter.

Members of the bomb disposal squad removing a large unexploded device after the heavy bombing of Plymouth.

bombs. A large proportion of the premises owned by the society were already being patrolled by voluntary fire-watchers.

Non-stop dance music was played by two bands at the Pier Pavilion on Plymouth Hoe. The joviality kept people's spirits up, although on 9 January the city had its 247th alert.

The bombing of Plymouth

On 11 January 1941 the Wolsdon Street bomb in Plymouth, which was one of the biggest unexploded bombs dropped on the city, was removed by the disposal squad. It had been there since the raid of 28 December 1940. It weighed over a ton and was 9ft long with fins another 2ft.

On 13 January Plymouth had its 256th alert. The raid, which lasted three hours, started at 6pm and resulted in the deaths of twenty-six people. Another fifty-five were seriously injured and sixty-two were slightly injured. A shelter at Madeira Road took a direct hit and many people were trapped. The attack involved twenty-five aircraft and 106 high explosive bombs were dropped. The damage was widespread.

The *Western Morning News* of Saturday 25 January reported on a bombed hospital in Plymouth. A high explosive bomb had scored a direct hit on the women's ward and

The Maternity Ward of the City Hospital, Plymouth. Bombing raids took their toll on the city hospitals and many casualties had to be cared for in adapted premises outside the city. Hardly a hospital in the city escaped damage. Those affected included the Royal Naval Hospital at Stonehouse, Greenbank, Lockyer Street and Devonport, the Royal Eye Infirmary at Mutley and the Isolation Hospital at Swilly.

another fell near the kitchens. These, however, caused only temporary inconvenience. 'All the staff worked very well and overcame the difficulties,' an official said. 'There was no serious interference with the feeding or the hospital work. True, a certain amount of redistribution of patients was necessary. We had some incendiary bombs, which were all extinguished by members of the various staffs, from doctors to workmen.'

Only two of the staff were injured, one was soon discharged and the other was recovering well. A nurse who suffered from burns made a complete recovery. Although one patient was killed, other patients and nurses had miraculous escapes. The bomb went right through the ward and exploded underground. Four patients were on the partially collapsed upper floor. Penned in a corner, they were unhurt, despite their portion of the floor being suspended in mid-air. Covered with debris, the patients were carried down a damaged fire escape by members of the staff. 'It was fortunate that the women's ward was not full,' said the official, 'patients in damaged wards were taken to wards that had not suffered. In fact, we were ready for receiving air-raid casualties from outside, and did get some that night. Some were operated on at once. Altogether we can say we were soon functioning normally,' he concluded.

On 27 January 1941, there was a huge explosion at Coxside in Plymouth when an attempt to reconnect the gas supply was unsuccessful. Three men were killed and five were injured and ominous bulges were noticed in Union Street caused by broken gas mains.

At the beginning of February, able seaman Thornton Thomas, of Cothill, Station Road, Ilfracombe, told the *North Devon Journal* how he was saved after his ship, the SS *West Wales* was torpedoed:

'In the darkness, I was swimming about in the great waves of the Atlantic after being torpedoed and I offered a prayer to God that he would send me something to float on, my prayer was answered quickly. A raft came. I clung to it. I was saved.'

Mr Thomas continued:

'It was in the darkness of the morning when we received our first hit from a torpedo. It struck the ship's bow. We hardly had time to lower the boats before we were hit again amidships. Then I heard a voice cry "Tom, Tom," it was a 16-year-old member of the crew. He was calling to me. I drifted to him and pulled him aboard. A few minutes later we picked up an Indian fireman and got him aboard the raft. The ship had gone down. I did not know what had become of the skipper, he would not leave the ship. At daybreak we were picked up by a destroyer.'

The ship's master 46-year-old Captain Frederick C. Nicholls, of Instow, Devon, lost his life as well as fifteen others from a crew of thirty-seven. They were on their way with Convoy SC19 from New York and Halifax to Newport when they were torpedoed by *U-94*.

Vital supplies such as gas and electricity were in short supply for many households in Devon. Obtaining a bag of coal had become almost impossible. In Plymouth, the drinking water supplies had been affected by the bombing and water carts were sent out to some areas of the city.

On 5 February the Air Training Corps was formed to provide teenagers and young men with flying experience. Many later joined the RAF.

On 13 February 1941 ten enemy planes, returning from a raid on Cardiff, attacked Plymouth. Bombs fell on Stoke and on Millbay. One fell on the roadway outside the Continental Hotel where there had been a large dance. The hotel was badly damaged but luckily, there were only a few casualties. At Ford, however, three houses were destroyed and eleven people were killed when they became trapped. The early morning raid meant that most people were caught in their beds. During the raid, two bombs fell within the grounds of the Royal Eye Infirmary at Mutley. Luckily, they didn't explode.

Children arriving at Exeter after being evacuated from Bristol towards the end of February.

The smiling faces of evacuee children who arrived by train at Brent Station during February.

The children being registered.
A nurse can be seen checking
their health cards.

During February, it was announced that children from Bristol were to be evacuated to Devon. They were soon to leave the city for an indefinite stay in the country. Under the Bristol evacuation scheme, children between the ages of 5 and 14 in certain parts of the city were to be sent to Devon within the following fortnight. It was expected that the actual evacuation would take four days to complete. About 500 voluntary workers as well as 240 Bristol school teachers would accompany the children and see them safely to their billets, but only the teachers would remain with them.

On 15 February, a German Heinkel III crashed in a field at Higher Luscombe near Totnes killing all on board. The plane had previously been hit by British fighters further up the coast.

More than fifty German bombers dropped high explosives around Valletort Road, Stoke in Plymouth on 19 February. Bombs were also dropped near to Stonehouse Town Hall. Damage was caused to property and one person died of their injuries. The raiders headed off towards South Wales.

Homes for evacuees
Later in February the Ilfracombe Evacuation Committee decided to start proceedings against twenty-five local householders who had defied billeting orders. The householders were called to attend the next Petty Sessional Court. Several well-known townspeople were summoned. Since the beginning of February some 400 evacuee children from Bristol had arrived in the town. At first, it was thought that sufficient voluntary billets could be located for them but only eighty voluntary homes were found. Consequently, compulsory orders were enforced and billeting notices duly issued. In the meantime, many people hurried to the Evacuation Office to present their case why they were unable to accommodate children. In some cases, the facts were substantiated but in the majority, the excuses were trivial. When they were told that children would be brought to them at a certain time, defiance was shown even before the children arrived.

On the arrival of the first batch of children, most were placed in happy homes. However, there were a few who had been taken to homes only to find on their arrival that the doors were locked, even though the occupants were evidently at home. This occurred several times and the fact that the children were being brought back, and not wanted, was very upsetting to the children and to the officials. Mr F.G. Reed stated that he had that experience when he took three children to a home in the St Brannocks district. When he knocked at the door he received no response. He waited, but in vain. The children began to cry, but the timely help of a neighbour, who was already full, but managed to fit the children in, saved the day. In Mr Reed's own words, 'It made me weep.'

A further party arrived from Bristol a couple of days later. Fortunately, only seven out of the whole party were obliged to go to the hostel until homes could be found for them. Every child was eventually found a home.

Towards the end of February it was through the generosity of Miss Clara N. Harrington, of Minneapolis, USA, who had sent a cheque for £395 to the English-speaking union, Plymouth was to have another mobile canteen, which would be formally handed over for service on 7 March. The canteen was to be staffed by members of the WVS.

For the first time in the history of Lundy Island, a German plane crashed there and burst into flames. On the afternoon of Monday 3 March, islanders saw a bomber flying lower and lower until the swastika on its side was plainly visible. The plane then dived steeply and hit the ground in the parish of Littleham. Flames rapidly enveloped the tangled wreckage and the machine was soon burnt out. Five German airmen from the plane managed to escape and were soon rounded up by the islanders. They gave no trouble and were taken under guard in a navy patrol vessel, which in peacetime was the link between Instow and Lundy Island. They were landed at Appledore and then taken to Bideford where they left under escort for an unknown destination.

On 14 and 15 March 1941, six bombs fell on Central Park in Plymouth with two near to the Southern Railway at Devonport. Five people were killed in the bombing attacks and seven houses were demolished when six bombs fell on Royal Navy Avenue in Keyham. One thousand incendiary devices fell on the area which caused twenty-seven fires.

King George VI and Queen Elizabeth paid their first visit to Plymouth on 20 March. They had tea with Lord and Lady Astor at Elliot Terrace before their departure. Two hours later, the city suffered its worst and most devastating attack.

The *Western Independent* wrote after the bombing:

George Street, Plymouth, as full of life as it was never to be again. School children lined the pavements, waving Union Jacks. In the bright sunshine, a gleaming car passed. In it was the King and Queen. In the Guildhall Square, their Majesties inspected the ARP personnel. Westwell Street was thronged, one could not move. A memorable afternoon, followed by two nights of death and destruction. Nothing looked more tragic on the early morning of March 22nd than seeing George Street, where the King and Queen had driven through, become a street of blackened and misshapen ghosts.

The destruction of Plymouth

On the night of 20 March 1941, Plymouth experienced some of its heaviest bombing. The attack started at 8.39pm with the dropping of thousands of incendiary bombs and went on for four hours. Pathfinding flares were followed by an intensive wave of high explosives from many German bombers. The target for the attack was the centre of the city, including Stonehouse to Cattedown and Plymouth Hoe to Mutley.

There were many fires all over the city, the first major one being at the premises of Spooner's. Facing St Andrew's Church, it had been a main feature of Plymouth for many years. The whole area became a huge furnace and despite the efforts of firemen, it was impossible to save it. A further fire gutted the Royal Hotel near to Derry's Clock and stopped short of the recently built Royal Cinema. The city was obliterated and unrecognisable. Fire brigades from all areas of Devon rushed to assist Plymouth as did the police and thousands of members of the Civil Defence forces. Members of the Army, Navy and Royal Air Force all assisted but were overwhelmed by the ferocity of the attack.

On the morning of 21 March 1941 as daylight broke, Plymouth lay destroyed and blackened, a shadow of its former self. The attack was repeated again later that

Derry's Clock in Plymouth still standing after the bombing of 20 March 1941. The Bank Chambers, now the Bank Public House, can be seen on the right of the picture. The sign fixed to the right of Derry's Clock says, 'To the Hoe' and points towards Lockyer Street.

Looking towards George Street and the Prudential Buildings in Plymouth. The Western Morning News *Building can be seen in the background. The building survived mainly because it had only been built two years previously and was made with solid, fire proof building material. There was an underground bunker for the workers beneath the building.*

day and Plymouth suffered another pounding from the Luftwaffe. The Guildhall, St Andrew's Church and the Municipal buildings were all gutted by fire. The Guildhall was later earmarked for demolition but it was eventually rebuilt and re-opened in 1959.

In the two intensive attacks on the 20 and 21 March, 336 people in Plymouth lost their lives. Five further attacks in April brought the toll to 590.

There was hardly a building in Plymouth that wasn't touched in some way by the blitz. Much of the city centre was obliterated and although many buildings remained amongst the debris, most were damaged beyond repair.

Many of the most popular streets including Bedford Street, Union Street, Old Town Street, Frankfort Street, Cornwall Street and George Street were either totally destroyed or severely damaged. Major buildings were obliterated and schools were also hit. These included Plymouth High School for Girls, the Hoe Grammar School and the infants school at Summerland Place. Many churches were destroyed also including St James the Less, King Street Methodist, St Peter's, George Street Baptist. The bombing was indiscriminate and devastating.

A policeman directs people away from the Royal Sailors' Rest at Fore Street, Devonport. Three men from the Civil Defence survey the damage in the background. The building was better known as 'Aggie Weston's.' With its destruction went 777 beds which had been occupied each night since the beginning of the war. The canteens and kitchens there had provided 2,000 meals every day.

Drake Circus in Plymouth. On the left, amongst the rubble, are signs directing people to the destroyed shops' new premises probably nearby or in Mutley which was to become the main shopping area in the city. Mutley had lost out to the shops of the busy city centre before the bombing but after the blitz, it became the city's primary shopping centre and home of many destroyed businesses.

Costers store on fire in Frankfort Street, Plymouth. Costers was a clothing and general department store. They were well known for their school uniforms.

A policeman surveying the damage in Union Street, Plymouth. The badly damaged shop on the right is 'Weaver to Wearer', the 30 shillings tailors. They also had a shop where the old Criterion Cinema had been in Cornwall Street.

Plymouth Co-operative Society's headquarters in Frankfort Street. The building, on the corner of Frankfort Street and Courtney Street, was a major landmark in the city centre with a clock tower, standing 120 feet. When the building was bombed on the night of 21 March 1941, only the tower, shown here, and parts of the walls remained.

Searching for bodies amongst the rubble in Plymouth. During the raids of 20 and 21 March 1941, 336 civilians were killed. The further heavy bombing in April resulted in another 590 being killed. On top of this, thousands were injured. Many people were reported missing and no trace of them was ever found.

The destroyed Cornwall Street in Plymouth. After the blitz, Ivor Dewdney was the first shop to be built in the new Cornwall Street. Their first pasty shop before the war was at 2 King Street. Shops in the old wrecked Cornwall Street became known as bungalow shops because there was nothing upstairs.

St Andrew's Church in Plymouth after being bombed. St Andrew's Cross, which stood outside, was thought to be unstable and was demolished as being unsafe. The main chancel became a garden and flowers were planted around the pillars.

Looking towards George Street from George Place, Plymouth. Some very official men look around in disbelief at the remains of the city. The building in the background belonged to the American Shoe Company. George Street had been the main thoroughfare of pre-war Plymouth.

Derry's Clock on the junction of George Street and Bank of England Place, Plymouth. The sign in the foreground, illuminated by the fire behind, stood above the underground toilets. Derry's Clock was, before the war, considered to be the centre of Plymouth. All trams and buses terminated nearby. It was also a well-known meeting place and it was said that 'marriages may be made in Heaven but in Plymouth, they're arranged under Derry's Clock.'

The shell of Plymouth Guildhall. Here, it's possible to see the total devastation caused to the inside of the Guildhall. On 21 March 1941, the Guildhall, St Andrew's Church and the Municipal buildings were gutted by fire after intensive bombing and although the Guildhall was earmarked for demolition, it was eventually rebuilt and re-opened in 1959.

The blitzed George Street in Plymouth. Such was the unbelievable heat that thick plate glass windows melted in pools onto the pavement. Gold in a jeweller's shop turned to liquid and trickled away. Tins of meat and soup exploded and where they were packed together, they fused into lumps of molten tin.

The remains of Drake Circus, Plymouth. The building on the left housed the Liverpool Victoria Insurance Offices. A huge hoarding advertising Bovril covered the right hand side of the building. Many of the buildings still standing would later be torn down for redevelopment.

The remains of Charles Church in Plymouth. It still stands at Charles Cross roundabout as a memorial to Plymouth's war dead. Charles Church was situated in Vennel Street until the area was obliterated by heavy bombing. The Council's reconstruction committee decided to demolish the church on 15 June 1953 but it was saved and, on 1 November 1958, the Reverend J. Allen James dedicated it as a memorial to the 1,200 civilians who lost their lives in the war. Alderman G. Wingett, the Lord Mayor, unveiled a plaque on the North wall.

In the dockyard, the bombing was bad but not as damaging as it could have been and within a few months, it was back to 90 per cent efficiency. Outside the city, the bombing was just as bad and areas affected included Devonport, Stonehouse, St Budeaux, Swilly and Saltash Passage. Devonport lost many buildings including the Post Office, the Alhambra Theatre, the Synagogue, the Hippodrome and the Salvation Army Headquarters. Homes that were either destroyed or beyond repair amounted to 3,754; others that were seriously damaged but able to be repaired amounted to 18,398; Houses that were slightly damaged amounted to an additional 49,950.

After the heavy bombing over the two nights of 20 and 21 March, Naval ratings from HMS *Raleigh* were given the grim task of recovering the 292 bodies from the ruins. Lord Astor requested that if he was killed during enemy action that he should have no special ceremony and be buried alongside his fellow Plymothians.

A soldier and his wife with Lady Astor in Plymouth. The Astors regularly visited the various shelters set up around the city for people who had lost their homes. She wrote to one friend, 'Plymouth looks like Ypres – only worse. There is so much to do that I sometimes think I'll be here forever.'

This photo shows some of the devastation that was felt all over Plymouth. Here, many buildings still stand but most are damaged and would become victims of later bombing raids. All over the city, bomb disposal squads worked coolly and efficiently dealing with the many unexploded bombs. At Osborne Place on the Hoe, one large bomb was being removed on a lorry when it exploded killing five men.

The destroyed pier, Plymouth Hoe. The pier looks in a sorry state after being destroyed by the many bombs that fell on Plymouth in 1941. The blitzed pier remained until the end of 1952 when the council announced that they wanted to get rid of it as soon as possible.

Many children were packed off to live with relatives, friends or obliging families in safe areas in the countryside. Thousands left on special trains which many saw as an adventure while others were upset to leave their parents behind. Lady Astor said at the time, 'What helped the evacuation was that everyone seemed to have a cousin in the country!'

News of the devastation of Plymouth soon reached the rest of the world and gifts arrived from all over particularly the United States who sent ambulances, soft toys, food packages and surgical dressings. The Royal Sailors Rest received crates of supplies so large that they were unable to get them into the building.

The *Western Morning News* of Friday 21 March reported on the King and Queen's further visit to Plymouth:

'We are keeping our chins up, your majesty,' said the air raid warden of a bombed Plymouth street yesterday, standing amid the debris of his home. 'Well done,' said the Queen. 'It is only by keeping our chins up, as we are doing, that we shall win the war.'

Such was the spirit that Plymouth noted and admired, and such was the spirit of Plymouth that obviously moved the King and Queen yesterday during

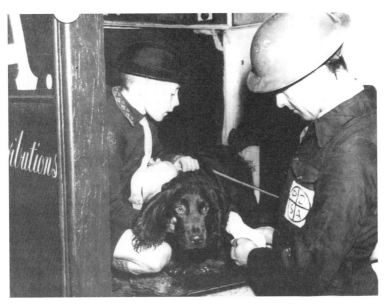

The Animal Rescue Squad. Maria Dicken founded the PDSA in 1917 to provide care for animals whose owners couldn't afford their vet's bills. The PDSA had their own animal rescue squad that worked along side Civil Defence Workers. Many animals were trapped and injured during the blitz and dogs were used to find them. Many animals were awarded the Dicken Medal which the press called, 'The Animals' VC'.

Children queue with their pets for them to be inspected by the Animal Rescue Squad. Many animals were overcome with fright during the raids. Here, a vet carefully checks a cocker spaniel while children look on. One boy even has his own tin hat to protect himself against the falling debris and rubble.

A couple save all they can from their bombed house. This consists of mainly sheets and blankets. With many of the large stores which supplied the bulk of food and clothing destroyed, supplies were short and were rushed to the city from other parts of the country.

their intensive tour of the city that began in the early morning and did not end until the evening. News of the visit had been kept a secret, for the tour was informal. Yet hardly had their Majesties started through the streets than cheering crowds lined the footpaths, and Union flags of all sizes twinkled from the hands of adults and children alike. Though the Royal Navy had its own special type of welcome for His Majesty, it was amid the homes torn and blasted by Nazi bombs that hearts were opened to King and Queen. Faces that were smiling and happy, despite the deeper lines of worries caused by bombing, testified to the magnificent morale of the citizens. As the car with the Royal insignia moved slowly through the streets, cheers rolled upon cheers in deafening waves.

The Queen talked to an elderly couple who had lived in their house for 36 years, Mr and Mrs E.J. Heap, of 15, Nanpean Street. On being told that they had neither gas nor water, Her Majesty turned to them and said, 'Really has everything been broken then?' Lady Astor, who accompanied the Queen, interjected: 'Not quite, Ma'am, their spirit is unbroken.'

Plymouth's first war widow was presented to the King and Queen at Cattedown. When the Queen was told that Mrs Violet Burring, of 56 Laira Bridge Road, had lost her husband three days after war broke out, Her Majesty said, 'I am so sorry.' Mrs Burring was carrying Maureen, youngest of her four children, who was born soon after her father's death. The queen tweaked the child's arm and said smilingly, 'Isn't she sweet?' Maureen flashed an answering smile, then shyly hid her face against her mother's neck. The King asked Mrs Burring about her husband, and she replied that he had been serving in the Navy. 'Have you got a job?' queried the King. 'Yes sir, I am working to keep my kiddies,' Mrs Burring said. That's fine,' remarked His Majesty in a tone of admiration.

The warm friendliness the King and Queen instilled in the people with whom they talked was impressive. During their Majesties' afternoon tour, an air raid occurred but the programme continued as if nothing had happened. The people who had crowded the streets to cheer the Royal visitors did not move and the raid passed without incident.

The fire brigade practising their drill. Until the National Fire Service was reorganised in the middle of 1941, fire brigades were a local concern. This meant that the fire brigade was part of the police force and came under the command of the Chief Constable and the Plymouth City Council. It was completely efficient for normal fire fighting but totally unequipped for the devastation caused by the blitz.

Towards the end of March, it was announced that the total for Ilfracombe's War Weapons Week stood at £66,422 towards the £100,000 aimed for. Exmouth, whose objective was also £100,000, had raised £139,894.

On 24 March, Countess Fortescue, the wife of the Lord Lieutenant of Devon, was among those who registered for testing as voluntary blood donors at the North Devon Athenaeum in Barnstaple, on the opening day of North Devon's blood transfusion week on behalf of the Army Blood Transfusion Service. About 200 registered at the North Devon Athenaeum, which was the Barnstaple registration centre, as blood donors and the authorities expressed themselves well pleased with the results of the first day's appeal. Included in the 200 were a number of foreign refugees from Barnstaple and the surrounding neighbourhood. At the Tyrell Cottage Hospital, which was Ilfracombe's registration centre, a similar number registered.

During March, a Devon fisherman roped a mine. Tom Newton was awarded the Medal of the Civil Division of the OBE for mooring a floating mine and for saving a bridge and the lives of a number of cottagers. In an official announcement of the award, Newton's address was given only as 'Devon'.

Mr Newton said, 'I was going down to the beach early one morning when I saw the mine bobbing about in the sea on an incoming tide and within a few yards of

Brave men of the Bomb Disposal Squad moving one of the many explosives that fell on Plymouth but failed to go off. From the time France fell to Germany in June 1940, the Germans had access to closer aerodromes to Britain. From here, they launched their attacks on the South West.

the bridge. It seemed to me that it was likely to strike the bridge in a few minutes and that the bridge might go sky high. My wife was standing on the parapet and she wanted to assist me in securing the mine, but I told her to go back to the cottage. I went into the water and guiding the mine with an oar, secured it with a rope after a couple of attempts. I then towed it about 100 yards down the river, where I moored it. The authorities came later and dealt with it and that's all there was in it.'

Evacuated children from London in Devon were learning to till the soil. It was reported that several boys who had reached school leaving age had found jobs on farms, as well as in a sawmill and cider factory at Totnes, South Devon. One of the boys said; 'I don't think I'll go back to London when this lot's over. Its the country for me now.'

On Monday 24 March, local newspapers reported on the task of cleaning up in Plymouth. The city had settled down to the grim business of cleaning up after its two days of successive night raids. It was announced that the Deputy Regional Commissioner, General Lindsay, had visited the city, made investigations, and given the authorities advice. Women toured the bombed city in loud-speaker vans announcing where feeding facilities could be found. They also offered financial relief to the homeless.

The men of the bomb squad surrounded by unexploded bombs.

Lady Astor inspects the bomb damage, accompanied by a civil defence worker. Lady Astor was born in America in 1879. She married Waldorf Astor in 1906 and they lived at 3 Elliot Terrace on the Hoe. She was the MP for Sutton from 1919 to 1945.

Two firemen survey the damage done to the Guildhall. The Auxiliary Fire Service was formed at the beginning of the war to assist the regular fire brigades. Many of the ranks were made up of women and throughout the country, there were 32,200 women serving in the National Fire Service. Many were part timers, men were on duty every fourth night and women every sixth night.

The Navy helping with moving salvaged furniture and belongings. On the side of the lorry, it reads, 'We shift you quicker than a dose of Epsoms!' All salvaged furniture was carefully labelled before storing so it could be traced back to its owners.

Women salvage workers help man the hoses. In June 1938, the Women's Voluntary Service for Air Raid Precaution was formed. To begin with, the membership was essentially middle class and their uniforms consisted of bottle-green coats and hats which the volunteers had to pay for themselves.

Two boys try on helmets that they've found amongst the blitzed debris. A favourite pastime amongst children was to search for souvenirs amongst the rubble. Helmets or other military related items would be sought after but it could prove a dangerous hobby with unstable buildings and many unexploded bombs lying around.

The Lord Mayor's Hut Buffet at North Road Railway Station, Plymouth. All members of the HM services were welcome and could expect something warm to eat and a cup of tea. Work had started on rebuilding the station in 1938 but this had been interrupted by the war and it had to wait until 1956 before the work was restarted.

The Navy salvage force. A sign on the wall reads, 'Raw material for war material'. Everything was saved and here, Navy personnel sort items into containers marked, 'Paper', 'Iron' and 'Rags'. Anything that could be salvaged was and if possible, it was used again.

Lady Astor looks on as women salvage workers clear the rubble. Nöel Coward said of Lady Astor, 'Nobody who saw Lady Astor, as I did, when Plymouth was being bombed almost out of existence, could feel anything but profound and affectionate admiration. I remember in 1942 walking with her through the streets after a bad blitz. She dashed here, there and everywhere, encouraging, scolding, making little jokes. In the sitting room of one pathetic house, the roof and kitchen of which had been demolished, she ordered a pale young man to take the cigarette out of his mouth, told him he would ruin his lungs and morals with nicotine, slapped him on the back, and on we went.'

Salvage workers help to demolish the ruins in Plymouth. The Women's Voluntary Service was responsible for organising salvage drives which included the removal of railings. They also collected aluminium pots and pans, jelly moulds, kettles, paper and rubber and even artificial limbs. Much of this was never re-used but the drives brought together people and raised morale.

Girls of the Salvage Service. Salvage workers removed anything that could be saved and perhaps used again. Everything was in short supply so as much as possible had to be saved. On the floor is a Kodak box with many photos strewn around so perhaps this was the premises of one of Plymouth's many photographers.

Lady Astor talks to two workers in Plymouth. Lady Astor was well-known for her straight to the point way of talking. She had once said to Winston Churchill, 'If I was your wife I would give you poison!' to which Churchill replied, 'If I was your husband, I'd drink it!'

Thousands received free meals. For more than forty-eight hours, demolition and salvage parties worked almost continually to unearth the dead and buried under debris. They also recovered important documents. Thousands of people escaped injury due to the speed in which they took cover but a number of children under ten were killed during the bombing.

Naval authorities fed and helped the homeless and provided large supplies of foodstuffs from their own stores. The military lent cooking stoves so that others could enjoy a Sunday dinner. Evacuation of some of the civilian population in trains and buses to other parts of Devon eased the task of the authorities and enabled the emergency feeding plan to run smoothly.

Centres were quickly made available for the homeless and a 'Help your Neighbour' scheme was put into practice. Eleven centres for the homeless were available but fewer than 200 made use of the temporary homes. Some spent the night in fields and under hedgerows before trekking back to the city in the early hours.

Towards the end of March, in connection with the North Devon Blood Transfusion Week, an appeal for volunteers was made by the Vicar of Barnstaple (the Reverend F.M. Wallington) in his sermon at Barnstaple Parish Church.

Collecting salvage from a bombed home in Plymouth. Regular salvage drives were organised to help the war effort. Tin, rubber, iron, steel, paper, cooking fat and even silk stockings were all collected. A popular poster during the war read, 'Salvage saves Shipping'.

The mass grave at Efford, Plymouth. After the heavy bombing over the two nights of 20 and 21 March 1941, Naval ratings from HMS Raleigh were given the grim task of recovering the 292 bodies from the ruins. Lord Astor requested that if he was killed during enemy action that he should have no special ceremony and be buried alongside his fellow Plymothians.

Blitz victims buried

The *Western Morning News* of Friday 28 March reported on the burial of the victims of the blitz. The Bishop of Plymouth at the communal funeral at Efford Cemetery stated, 'We are gathered here as a united, family, without distinction of class, party, profession, occupation, or creed, to offer our deepest and most loving sympathy and our comfort to those who mourn.'

The coffin-filled grave was shrouded with the red, white and blue of the national flag. On one side were the mourners, and on the other, was a huge bank of flowers. At one end there were civic and other representatives.

In its tribute, the city was joined by all three Services. The commander-in-chief, with some of his staff officers, represented the Royal Navy, the Army was represented by the GOC of the area, and the RAF by the senior officer of the district. Many other organisations, including those concerned with civil defence, were also represented.

Those present included the Lady Mayoress (Lady Astor, MP), the Deputy Lord Mayor and Deputy Lady Mayoress (Alderman and Mrs W.J.W. Modley), the Town Clerk (Mr C. Campbell), Alderman L.R. Dunstan, Messrs. J. Churchward and S. Stephens, members of the Emergency Committee, Lord Mildmay of Flete, Lady Dunbar-Nasmith, the city engineer (Mr J. Paton Watson), and the city treasurer (Mr J. Ainsworth).

The Bishop said in his address:

We grieve over their loss and we ask ourselves to what purpose is all this waste, this sacrifice, this destruction. And then we bow our heads and we remember how we are taught by the Bible, and by our whole religion, that God achieves His purpose not only through active work and sacrifice, but through passive suffering, and quite humbly and quite certainly, we believe that those who have passed to Him showed patience and fortitude and bravery and have done their part for the regeneration of the world.

Brigadier A. Gye, of the Salvation Army, read a passage of Scripture, and the Vice-President of the Free Church Council, the Reverend W.D. Campbell, led the prayers. Then the Vicar of St Andrew's (the Reverend C.A. Martin) asked all those present to join in the Lord's Prayer. The Bishop and others stood while the Vicar-General of the Roman Catholic Diocese (the Right Reverend Mgr. F.C. Mahoney) began to read the funeral service. The simple ceremony closed with the blessing. Among the wreaths was one of tulips, irises and daffodils from the Lord Mayor and Lady Mayoress of Plymouth (Lord and Lady Astor). Another was from the staff of Plymouth Corporation in memory of a bus conductress. Many people laid bunches of spring flowers on the bank.

The newspaper reported that nurses of the children's ward of a Plymouth hospital were still with their little charges in death. Killed together in the ward when it was devastated by a high explosive bomb, they were buried in adjoining graves at Efford Cemetery. Only a few yards away was the communal grave. The committal service was conducted by the chaplain of the hospital. Union flags lined the graves, into which relatives and nurses dropped bunches of flowers including violets, roses and daffodils. Afterwards the graves were piled high with spring flowers. The relatives received the sympathy of the Lady Mayoress and the chaplain, who moved among them.

The Lady Mayoress was accompanied at the ceremony by the Deputy Lord Mayor and Deputy Lady Mayoress. Together with eight nurses in their white uniforms and navy and scarlet capes were officials of local hospitals, the city MOH (Dr T. Peirson), and Alderman F.D. Baxter, chairman of the Public Health Committee. The nurses buried were Miss Olivia May Willing, aged 19, of Trowbridge, Churchstow, Kingsbridge; Miss Monica White, aged 17, of 32, Broad Walk, Heston, Middlesex and Miss Lydia Rebecca Walters, aged 16, of 21, Penrose Street, Plymouth.

The five nights of heavy raids in April 1941 covered 23 hours and 16 minutes of continuous bombing and 1,140 high explosive bombs were dropped together with thousands of incendiaries. Altogether, 1,500 homes were demolished or destroyed beyond repair while another 16,500 were left damaged.

Fire fighting practice. The greater part of Plymouth burnt to the ground during the blitz of March and April 1941 because the local brigades had inadequate resources to tackle the many fires that broke out. Many brigades from other parts of the country rushed to Plymouth's aid but then found that their equipment wasn't compatible with that of the city's. This led to devastating consequences and many of the brigades had to stand idle.

Millbay Station, Plymouth, at the east end showing two bomb craters.

Damage after the bombing of Millbay Station, Plymouth. Here, members of the Navy help to clear away the debris. The railings were saved for the war effort.

Millbay Station was severely damaged by the bombing of March and April 1941 and was closed on 23 April 1941 after which the platform lines were only used for goods traffic loading.

The *Western Morning News* of Thursday 3 April carried a story about orphaned children in Plymouth:

Authorities who know that some children have lost either one or both of their parents are wondering what has become of these young people. From all parts of England and Wales offers are pouring in to adopt those 'kiddies' who are without homes or parents. Already many children have been billeted or temporarily adopted, but at the moment there are more homes than children. People have written to the Lady Mayoress, (Lady Astor), the Council of Social Service, the MOH, (Dr T. Peirson) and the billeting officer, offering permanent homes to any children who need them. Many of these people are, judging from the letters, of middle and working class, who had to work hard to make homes for themselves. All these offers are being dealt with at Beaumont Hut, Beaumont Park, Plymouth. An official said yesterday that a father, who perhaps has been left with one or more children if the mother is killed, or a mother, who is left a widow with a large family, can apply for a home for one of their children if the home is gone and money is scarce. The adoption can be temporary or permanent.

Pophams advertising their wares after being bombed out in Plymouth. Before the blitz, shops such as Pophams, Dingles, Spooners and Yeos were all located in large adjoining buildings but after the bombing they were found operating in small shops from Mannamead to Drake Circus.

A man rummages through burnt books after the central library is destroyed. The library was opened on 25 October 1910. On 22 April 1941, the building and its books were severely damaged by bombing. Some books were rescued but most were destroyed in the fire. In August, the Lord Mayor, Lord Astor, reopened the library on a temporary basis, in the museum.

This also applies to relatives who may have taken a child whose parents are both dead or missing, or perhaps whose father is on active service. Already many anxious and now grateful parents have brought their youngsters to Beaumont Hut because their homes have been wrecked. They have found good homes for them for a while until they can establish a more normal means of living.

On 8 April hundreds of incendiary devices were dropped on the Hartley, Mannamead, Mutley, Lipson, Beaumont Road and Friary areas of Plymouth. About thirty fires were cause by the devices but these were put out by the police, wardens and civilians. High explosive bombs fell on Swilly, damaging houses and injuring four people.

On 21 April more extensive raids commenced on Plymouth and fires raged all over the city. Widespread destruction took place similar to the attack a month previously. Military bases were hit and a bomb hit the public shelter at Portland Square killing seventy-two of its occupants.

On 22 April 1941, the Plymouth library and its books were severely damaged by bombing. Some books were rescued but most were destroyed in the fire.

The destroyed football stadium of Plymouth Argyle, the victim of a night raid in April 1941.

Another victim of a night-time raid in April 1941 was Plymouth Argyle's football ground. The ground was thought to be a safe area, so much so that a large amount of furniture and pianos salvaged from people's homes was stored there. Unfortunately, these were all destroyed in the fires that engulfed the ground. The site was thought to be less vulnerable because it was away from the city centre.

The raids and heavy bombing of Plymouth continued until the end of the month devastating the city.

On 29 April 1941, the GWR locomotive 4911, 'Bowden Hall', was paused during an air raid when a bomb fell so near to it that it was damaged beyond repair.

The *Western Morning News* of Wednesday 30 April reported that four German bombers had been shot down in Monday night's raid on Plymouth. One was destroyed by fighter planes and one was shot down by AA fire and crashed into the sea only 200 yards from the shore. When it hit the water, it threw up a terrific column of spray. A search was made at daybreak for wreckage but the quicksands where it crashed had swallowed it up. The raid was on a heavy scale for a time, a large number of enemy planes being engaged. Oil bombs, as well as high explosives and thousands of incendiaries, were dropped indiscriminately in a residential district and flares lit up the scene. Flashes from the anti-aircraft barrage, which was heavy, were continuous. There were a number of casualties, including some dead. A first aid post was hit and there were several fires. Houses were demolished and men, women and children were

*On 29 April
1941 the GWR
locomotive 4911,*
Bowden Hall, *was
paused during an
air raid when a
bomb fell so near
to it that it was
damaged beyond
repair.*

*A Home Guard inspection in Plymouth. Between April and May 1941, there were 330 full
time wardens and 1,406 part-time wardens. During just five nights in April, the casualties
in the Civil Defence included 40 killed and 120 injured. In 1941, an order stated that
all males between the ages of 16 and 60, if not in the Home Guard or helping with Civil
Defence, had to do 48 hours fire watching duty a month.*

The Navy lends a hand with clearing up. Here, they can be seen in Fore Street, Devonport, just about to pass the remains of the Forum Cinema. The Navy, when land based, also helped women of the WVS cook stew for the many homeless people.

killed and maimed. Digging was in progress at the rear of one house where people were thought to be in an Anderson shelter. One man left a shelter to deal with an incendiary bomb and was killed when a high explosive dropped close to him. 'It was a living hell out here for about half an hour,' said one person in a residential district. 'I was on the battlefield in the last war but have never seen or heard anything like it. We had to shout to each other to make ourselves heard with the din of barrage and bombs.

The German News Agency statement said: 'German bomber units last night attacked Plymouth with good effect. Heavy explosions, large fires visible a long way off, and numerous smaller fires were observed, particularly among the harbour installations.'

The *Western Morning News* of Thursday 1 May carried an article about 'savage Nazi raids on Plymouth.' Casualties were heavy and the material damage was considerable. The raiders dropped showers of incendiaries and high explosives. Among the 'military objectives' hit were two hospitals, a home for old people, six shelters and a school. The Lord Mayor of Plymouth, in a message to Lord Woolton, the Minister of Food, referred to Plymouth as 'the worst blitzed town in England'. This was the second blitz on successive nights and the fifth intensive attack in nine nights.

Winston Churchill visited Plymouth on 2 May 1941. Churchill spent a long time touring the devastated city and he was deeply moved by what he saw.

Seven raiders were destroyed, three by night fighters and four by gun fire. The barrage set up by anti-aircraft units was terrific and at times the noise swamped even the sound of bursting bombs. The anti-aircraft gunners had one of their best nights on Tuesday. Crews at a gun site in the Plymouth area cheered when a German machine disintegrated in the air after they had fired a few rounds at it. Shore watchers saw another bomber dive into the sea and when a large enemy machine was hit in mid-air and blew up there was a great explosion which shook the ground.

Mr Leslie Hore-Belisha, MP for Devonport, toured the devastated areas of Plymouth on the following day. He was horrified at the mad fury of the attack. Mr Hore-Belisha said, 'I think the determination which is in the people's minds must impress those who are directing the war and impel them to the most dynamic action. I have never been prouder to represent Devonport than now, when the place is in this agony and my one desire is to help in any way I can.'

Winston Churchill was visibly upset as he toured Plymouth on 2 May 1941. 'Your homes are down but your hearts are high!' he told the people of Plymouth. His visit greatly boosted the people as he toured street after street of destroyed homes and businesses. Churchill spent a long time touring the devastated city and he was deeply moved by what he saw. Lady Astor told Churchill, 'It's all very well to cry, Winston, but you've got to do something!' His visit brought little

Winston Churchill in front of the Guildhall in Plymouth. Churchill was visibly upset as he toured the city on 2 May 1941.

improvement to the lives of the people living in Plymouth but it vastly improved morale. He left Plymouth by train and was met at Totnes before being taken to Dartmouth Naval College.

Al fresco dancing on the Hoe began in the first week of May 1941. It was a success from the beginning and the idea was first suggested by Lord Astor. Lady Astor was a frequent participant and among her partners was the Duke of Kent.

On 7 May 1941, the residents of Pomphlett had a narrow escape when a bomb destroyed three houses and damaged fifteen others. Three people were killed, however. They were the Reverend W. Spencer, a Naval man and a Plymouth businessman. Elsewhere in the city, bombs were dropped on Millbay, Thorn Park and Stoke but there were no casualties.

The *North Devon Journal* of Thursday 8 May carried a story under the headline CHANCELLOR CONGRATULATES BARNSTAPLE. The Mayor of Barnstaple (Alderman Charles F. Dart, JP) received a congratulatory telegram from the Chancellor of the Exchequer on the outstanding success of the Barnstaple area war weapons week. It read: 'My hearty congratulations and grateful thanks on the splendid success of your War Weapons week, Kingsley Wood.'

The Barnstaple area effort, which set out to raise £150,000, resulted in the subscription of £431,209, approximately £15 per head of the population. The BBC's

Left: Lady Astor dances with a sailor on Plymouth Hoe. Outside dancing on the Hoe commenced in the first week of May 1941.

Right: Lady Astor dancing with a soldier on the Hoe. Nöel Coward said at the time, 'After all that devastation, on a Summer evening, people were dancing on the Hoe. It made me cry. The bravery, the gallantry, the Englishness of it!'

Bomb damage at Pomphlett. Here a direct hit has demolished someone's home.

Children dancing on the Hoe. Many dance in groups as soldiers watch on. The dances drew people together and some people travelled from outlying areas to join in. In the background can be seen Drake's Island and to the right, Mount Edgcumbe.

A young girl sings with the army band at an open air concert on the Hoe. The dances continued for many years, although when they started, the bandstand was still in position. A huge dance was held on the Hoe to celebrate VE Day.

announcement of the result of War Weapons Weeks said that the West Country should be proud of Barnstaple's £431,000.

Another raid took place on Plymouth on 8 May. Three bombs and a paramine were dropped on Central Park in Plymouth but did little damage to the open space. At Plymstock, two people were killed and three were injured. Further scattered raids followed all over the West Country including one at Staddon Heights. Across the Tamar, bombs fell at Saltash and Torpoint.

During May, the Devon Air Squadron Fund, which aimed at providing a squadron of fighters for the RAF, raised a total of £25,000. This was sufficient to purchase five of the complete squadron of nine planes. The chairman of the fund, Mr J.W. Chesters, announced the total at an Exeter Rotary Club luncheon and he appealed for helpers at a flag day the following day.

On 11 May, bombs fell on Cobourg Street in Plymouth. A house was destroyed killing one person and injuring three others. People were trapped in an adjoining building but were later rescued. Bombs also fell on Beaumont Road and the St Judes area of the city. There were more scattered raids on Plymouth on 13 and 17 May.

Towards the end of May, it was announced that the Royal Devon and Exeter Hospital annual egg appeal had resulted in 30,020 eggs being collected and a total of £99 being received in donations.

Many men were sent to Plymouth to help with repairs. The story was reported in the *Western Morning News* of Saturday 31 May. It stated that more operatives had been imported into Plymouth to repair bombed houses. Nearly 2,500 workmen were engaged in the task and first-aid repairs to many thousands of houses had been completed. Many of the workmen were from as far afield as London and the Midlands. There had been a good response to the appeal for voluntary billeting but several hundred men had been accommodated in hostels. One of these hostels was described as being the equivalent of a hotel. Formerly a well-known institution, it was damaged during the raids and there was little more than a day in which to get it cleaned up and ready to accommodate the workers. Officially, the task was regarded as impossible but a number of women voluntarily conducted a giant spring clean. Not only was the place swept and scrubbed, but by the time the workmen arrived the tables

Sailors teaching their partners to dance the Palais Glide on Plymouth Hoe during May 1941.

were laid, even to vases of flowers and the beds were made. Feeding arrangements were first class and a wireless set and a billiard table had been given for the men's recreation.

Serious air raids on Plymouth diminished as members of the Luftwaffe were withdrawn from Northern France as Germany prepared to invade Russia.

Clothing was rationed from June 1941 and people were issued with booklets containing clothing coupons. People were told to 'make do and mend' so that clothing factories and their workers could instead produce munitions.

The *Western Morning News* of Friday 6 June carried a story under the headline PLYMOUTH PIGEONS VALUED AID TO THE RAF. It reported that Plymouth's pigeons on national service had escaped the German bomb attacks. The birds were performing valuable work, mainly in connection with the RAF, over distances of many miles from the city. After the first blitz on Plymouth, arrangements were made for a training centre somewhere in Cornwall. When the birds were collected, not one was missing from the baskets, although the previous night fires from incendiary bombs had been fought in many lofts. Mr H.C. Woodman, the president of the Plymouth and District Combine and chairman of the St Jude's Flying Club, told the *Western Morning News* that the local clubs were carrying on breeding good racing pigeons which were being raced from 60 to 400 miles:

'Most of the members of the St Jude's Flying Club and the Premier Flying Club are members of the local group of the National Pigeon Service,' he said, 'and they have supplied, through their pigeon officers, thousands of pigeons for the use of the government. Although trained under the most vile weather conditions, the birds have set up wonderful records of speed and endurance. They are a last life-line to our wonderful boys of the air-crews in the RAF section operating over the sea.'

During June, it was revealed that two fishermen from Plymouth had been machine-gunned by a German plane while carrying out their work. They had no means of protection and their bodies were found on their boat, *Pansy*, some time later.

In June, a Flag Day was held at Crediton to raise funds for the North Devon Convalescent Children's Home in Lynton. The total raised was £9 15s 3d.

Towards the end of June, an inter-company competition held by the 14th (Moorside) Battalion Devonshire Home Guard at Canonteign, Ashton. B Company (Chagford and Moretonhampstead), commanded by Major E.A. Courthope, was successful by two points beating their nearest rivals.

Snap-shooting at falling targets, occupation of defensive positions and machine-gun posts, bombing and map reading were included among the events.

A challenge cup, presented by the officer commanding (Lieutenant Colonel A.C. Luther) and officers of the headquarters staff, was handed to the winners by Lieutenant Colonel F.G. Hay, commanding the South Devon Home Guard, who praised the excellence of the work and called upon the men to redouble their efforts towards efficiency.

The *Western Morning News* of Saturday 28 June carried a story calling for more women volunteers. Devon Women's Land Army had grown to 300 but more recruits were needed for work in the county and elsewhere. The committee was anxious to assist with operations in Kent. The War Agricultural Committee of that county was looking to Devon to supply sixteen volunteers for work in threshing gangs of four. One member of each gang was to act as forewoman. She had to be capable of taking responsibility and would be paid at the rate of 41s a week. Other members would receive 36s. Payment would be made irrespective of weather and between the threshing; the volunteers would be employed either on farms or on land clearance and drainage work.

During the bombing on the night of 4 July 1941, the Hoe area in Plymouth came under attack. Bombs were also dropped on Hartley, Crownhill, Keyham, Laira, Devonport and Beacon Park on that night. Near the Hoe, the Windsor Arms and nearby houses received direct hits. Two families were completely wiped out. The explosion was so violent that it threw one man over the tree tops and his body was found 300 yards away.

On 9 July bombs were dropped on Devonport and two policemen were killed as they were sheltering in a doorway at Fore Street. Seven people were injured in the attack and eight were trapped under a building but were later rescued safely. On the same night, bombs fell near to Bere Alston which put the Southern Railway line out of action for several hours.

The *Western Morning News* of Friday 18 July carried the story of the death of a local man:

A young Plymouth radio engineer volunteered for service overseas with the RAF in order that a married man might be released, and was subsequently killed. This drama has been revealed by Mr and Mrs F.L. Vosper, of Nutley, Crawford Road, Stoke, who have been informed of the death of their youngest son, Mr Ronald Graham Vosper, serving as a radio engineer with the RAF on an African station. Aircraftman Vosper, who was 19, was educated at Ford school and at Johnston Terrace School, later joining his father's radio business in Russell Street. He was home on leave in March prior to volunteering for foreign service to take the place of a married man. He was well known in the Plympton area as a footballer.

During the summer, the RAF base at Harrowbeer became operational. It had been built using material from the blitz of Plymouth. The presence of the Royal Air Force grew in Devon and the Yelverton air field became a satellite of RAF Exeter.

During July, the Princess Royal, on a visit to the South West stayed at Castle Hill, Filleigh, as the guest of Earl Fortescue, Lord Lieutenant of Devon, and Countess Fortescue. Her Royal Highness, on several occasions drove to South Molton during her stay. She also inspected the ATS unit, under Mrs Case-Beale, the commandant at Ilfracombe. Her visit was a surprise to most of the inhabitants but she was given a rousing welcome. After being introduced to officers, the Princess Royal made an inspection of the ATS on the parade ground and later took the salute.

The *Western Morning News* of Monday 28 July mentioned an open-air service on Plymouth Hoe. Men and women of many dominations worshipped together on Plymouth Hoe on Sunday 27 July. Under the shadow of the city's war memorial, the vicar of St Andrew's (the Reverend C.A. Martin) preached an open-air sermon in the first of a series of interdenominational services which it hoped would be held regularly on the Hoe throughout the summer. One object of the services was to help bring congregations of blitzed churches together.

At the end of July it was announced that Yealmpton War Weapons Week had produced £18,365, which was £14,365 in excess of the original aim of £4,000. A surplus of 15s 5d was sent to the Devon Spitfire Fund.

Prisoners of War and a local heroes

On 31 July Marine L.T. Heathman, who had been reported missing some weeks previously, wrote home to Ilsington, near Newton Abbot, stating that he was a prisoner of war in Greece. Before the war, he was a well-known cricketer in South Devon and claimed many successes with his fast bowling.

A former member of the Adelphi Sports Club in Paignton, Arthur Williams (RASC), the only son of Mr and Mrs Williams, of Littlegate Road, Paignton, was reported a prisoner of war in Italian hands.

Meanwhile, Mrs B. Stoneman, of 39, Polsham Road, Paignton received notification that her husband, Driver Ernest John Stoneman (RASC), was a prisoner of war in Corinthia, Greece. He had been posted as missing on 28 April.

The *Exeter and Plymouth Gazette* of Friday 1 August reported that Okehampton and Tavistock fire chiefs were to be honoured. Bravery during the heavy air raids at Plymouth had earned decorations for the chiefs of Tavistock and Okehampton fire brigades. The British Empire Medal was awarded to Mr Harry Reginald Horne, chief engineer of Okehampton Fire Brigade. During an air attack on Plymouth, the tower of a high building caught fire and there was a danger of the fire spreading. The water main was damaged and Mr Horne, placing a pump at a crater in front of the building, ran a hose up to the top floor. He entered the roof space below the tower with a ladder and extinguished the fire. There was a danger of the lower part of the premises catching alight, in which event Horne's escape would have been cut off. Mr Horne was instrumental in saving the building and by his initiative, devotion to duty, and total disregard of personal safety, set a fine example to the men under his control.

The Order of the British Empire was conferred on Mr Richard George Andrews, the chief officer of Tavistock Fire Brigade. During an air raid the Tavistock Fire Brigade, under the command of Chief Officer Andrews, was sent to Plymouth, where several large shops were on fire. Mr Andrews worked lines of hose on to the roof of an adjacent property to prevent the spread of a fire. The heat was intense but he continued to explore and led his crew to advantageous positions. Mr Andrews and his crew remained at their post continuously for nine hours, in conditions of great danger. The chief officer showed great determination and perseverance and set a fine example to his men by his cheerful demeanour and disregard of personal safety. He succeeded in preventing the flames spreading and remained at his post until the fire was extinguished.

During August, Charles Edward Heale, a soldier who was at the time in a military hospital and was formerly of Willey's Avenue, Exeter, was granted a decree nisi by the President (Lord Merriman) in the Divorce Court on the ground of the misconduct of his wife, Mrs Winifred Gertrude Heale. He cited a man named Frank Strachan as co-respondent and the suit was uncontested. The case for the husband was that last March, he learned that his wife had been convicted of harbouring Strachan, who was alleged to be a deserter from the forces, and later he found that misconduct had taken place between them.

The *North Devon Journal* of Thursday 7 August appealed for more recruits for the Barnstaple Home Guard. It was reported that since its formation, remarkable progress has been made by the local company, which formed part of a battalion of the Devonshire Home Guard. The guard was a well-equipped and sizeable force. The immediate need at Barnstaple was for more men to make use of the up to date facilities now available. Men capable of giving various forms of leadership were particularly wanted to help cope with developments based upon the growing strength of the Guard. The local membership figures were very good and indicated the popularity of the defensive organisation.

The article stated:

It must be obvious to the community that with the drainage caused by call-ups, and especially the calling up for industry of the men in the early forties, the Home Guard finds it increasingly difficult to stabilise its arrangements. It is true that from a national point of view these removals are not necessarily losses to the Home Guard as a whole. The problem created is really a local one. The locality itself can provide a clear remedy by making sure that all gaps are speedily and efficiently filled. We are sure that when the eyes of the public are opened to the measure of achievement already attained there will be such a sense of gratitude to all concerned and such a sense of pride in the local response that the call for volunteers will be irresistible.

On 15 August, the Southern Command issued a special order to all area commanders asking them to co-operate to the fullest extent with helping farmers to get in their harvest. Local commanding officers were asked to keep in touch with farmers in their vicinity so that, if necessary, they could help with the direct loan of personnel or make arrangements for requests to be met from other units. The Army commander stated that assistance to farmers during the harvest was to be considered an urgent service. He added 'The important point to remember is that the harvest must be collected quickly and safely.'

On 18 August 1941 a single German bomber was shot down by the Royal Marines. It had been a wet and windy night and the visibility was poor. The plane was hit by anti-aircraft fire and crashed in flames at Gawton Wood near Bere Alston.

At the beginning of September it was reported that the jam ration was to stay. The increase in the jam ration to one pound a month was to remain until further notice, and not made for the month August only, the Ministry of Food emphasised.

Henry Stevens, a young corporal of the Royal Army Pay Corps, fell 400 feet to his death from the cliffs at Ilfracombe, North Devon, during September while attempting

A German plane shot down on Dartmoor. All four members of the crew were killed when the plane crashed and exploded.

to rescue a comrade in difficulties on the cliff face. The other soldier was trying to climb up from the beach and was rescued by police and coastguards with ropes.

The *Western Times* of Friday 5 September wrote about a parade of tanks at Exeter:

> The city enjoyed itself to the full as did the personnel of the Royal Armoured Corps, who, with 'Speed the Tanks' as a motto for the city's latest war effort, drove, 'Waltzing Matilda' and the two 'Valentines' now on tour, through the principal streets amidst delighted and cheering crowds. The Services' parade and march past, in which they took such prominent place, exceeded the expectation of most. A light armoured scout car preceded the three leviathans, which were accompanied by two huge truck-like tank transporters. There were also field guns, Bren gun carriers and equipment and trench mortars. Mounted city police headed the procession, there were two service bands and the Exeter British Legion Band, various service units, contingents of the 4th Devon Old Comrades, the Old Contemptibles, the British Legion, the Home Guard, Red Cross and St John Ambulance Brigade.

Towards the end of September, it was reported that Private Basil Gordon White, who was riding a motor cycle, came into collision with an Army truck on the Devon side of Polson Bridge, near Launceston and sustained fatal injuries.

Recruits to the Women's Land Army engaged on potato lifting on Devon farms during September.

At the inquest at Launceston, the Coroner (Mr G.G. Wilson) returned a verdict that Private White died from multiple injuries accidentally, no blame was attached to the driver of the truck. Evidence of identification was given by a captain, who said White, born in 1910, was a general labourer in civil life and had had considerable experience of motor cycle riding. A medical officer said that when he examined White, he found that he was suffering from a fracture of the skull and a compound fracture of the right wrist as well as multiple contusions. Death was due to shock caused by the injuries.

Private John Donovan said that he was driving a 15cwt truck from Launceston in the direction of Okehampton. He passed over Polson Bridge, at not more than 15 miles an hour, and saw a motor cyclist coming down the hill. Witness was two feet from the near side of the road; the motor cyclist was over the white line. Suddenly he heard a crash behind. He stopped and rushed back and found the injured man on the road, bleeding profusely. Replying to Inspector Derges of Tavistock, the witness said that he thought the motorcyclist was going so fast that he was unable take the corner.

The *Western Times* of Friday 26 September reported that Bideford was prepared for a gas attack after triumphantly coming through its gas exercise on the previous Thursday, the first to be held in North Devon. Ample warning of the exercise was given and many came along eager to test their respirators. Staffs of business premises came out wearing their respirators as the tear gas containers were discharged in five of the principal streets of the town. Hardly anyone was caught without a respirator. The joint fire brigades came into the gas area and gave a demonstration, Captain H.V. Cope, the sub-controller in charge of North Devon ARP directed the exercise in conjunction with Mr T. Burton, Bideford's honorary ARP organiser.

Jewel thief jailed

At the beginning of October, a former student at a theological college, a member of the China Inland Mission and Congregational minister, Raymond Emanuel Bradford Young, aged 40, was sentenced to a total of twelve months' imprisonment at Torquay. He received six months on a charge of stealing £40 in notes and jewellery to the total value of £492 from Mrs Florence Maria Bates at a Torquay hotel on January 31 and six months for stealing a quantity of jewels to the value of £37 between August 4 and 5 from a Torquay hotel, the property of Mrs Ernest Wood.

Young, whose address was given as HM Prison, Exeter, where it was stated he was already serving a sentence of two months, was alleged to have stayed at various hotels throughout the country from 1938 to 1940, from which he absconded without paying, often having committed thefts.

Superintendent T. Milford, following Young's plea of guilty on each charge, stated that Mrs Bates missed her jewellery and money from a shopping bag inside a locked cabin trunk in her hotel room on the night of 31 January. The police ascertained that the defendant, who had been occupying the room next to that of Mrs Bates in the hotel, had absconded that night without paying his bill.

Young, interviewed at Exeter on 26 September, made a statement admitting the offence, but maintained that the amount of money was only £26 and not £40. He said that he had unlocked the trunk with his own keys, which happened to fit it.

With regard to the second case, the matter had not been reported to the police by the loser, Mrs Wood, who thought that she had mislaid her jewels. It came to light during inquiries into another matter and it was ascertained that the defendant had stayed at the same hotel as Mrs Wood, occupying a room next door to her. He had made a statement to the police admitting the offence. The Superintendent added that the jewellery had been sold in various towns and by the time it was traced, nearly all of it had been broken up and melted down. A quantity to the value of £90 belonging to Mrs Bates had been recovered.

There were a number of outstanding charges to be taken into consideration, including the theft of jewellery to the value of £250 from a Bournemouth hotel and the incurring debts by fraud at various hotels.

The Superintendent said that Young, a married man with 10-year-old son, had gone to Canada at the age of 15. In 1919 he became a student at the Theological College, New Jersey. He returned to London in 1922, became a member of the China Inland Mission, and in 1923 went to China with the mission. From May 1929 until 1931 he held the position of pastor at the Congregational Church, Linfield. Sussex. Subsequently he held a similar position in Sandwich. He resigned owing to differences with influential members of his congregation.

During the next few years he found employment as a chauffeur and a labourer and was often on public assistance.

From 1938 to 1940, he stayed at hotels and boarding-houses, committing thefts and leaving without paying. In 1940, he had been sentenced to a total of 15 months' imprisonment on three charges, when twenty other cases had been taken into consideration.

The *Western Morning News* of Friday 3 October reported that a Yelverton Red Cross working party held an American tea and sale on the previous Wednesday in aid of funds to buy material and wool. The wife of the American consul at Plymouth, Mrs H.M. Wolcott, who performed the opening ceremony, said that the Red Cross, as a relief society during wars, was a very old organisation and always to the front in helping.

As far back as the Crimean War, England had had Florence Nightingale, and during the Civil War in the United States there was Clara Barton. After stating that 5,730 articles had already been dispatched, Mrs Wolcott said that she knew material from America, to be made into garments, had been received in Yelverton, and she was sure more would come. 'I can assure you,' she added, 'help is coming constantly and quickly now from America, so keep your courage high and carry on. We are all working together.'

On Friday 10 October, it was stated at a meeting at Barnstaple of supporters of the North Devon Infirmary, that the proceeds of the recent Hospital Week in aid of the Institution yielded £5.948. Part of the sum was to be used for the provision of a new operating theatre.

The *Western Morning News* of Monday 27 October carried a story under the headline GIRL AGED 14 TAKES BROTHER'S PLACE. It read:

A 14-year-old Ivybridge girl, Delsia Barnes, has chosen an unusual career. For the past three months, sitting beside Mr Baber, a well known saddler, at his bench in the corner shop in Ivybridge's main street, she has been learning the craft of a worker in leather and is proving an apt pupil. In this job, Delsia is 'doing her bit', for not only is she taking the place of a brother, who is a prisoner of war in Germany, but as Mr Baber pointed out, she is engaged in work of national importance in providing harnesses for the farmers' horses. Delsia has a good example to follow, for her brother, Douglas, now in the hands of the Nazis, was an expert, and won a certificate of merit at the Bath and West Show at Plymouth some years ago for a bridle he made. She told me she liked the work and expected to continue with it. She went to Ivybridge Council School before entering the harness making business. Delsia, who is the younger daughter of Mr and Mrs J.H. Barnes, of 5, Bridge Park, Ivybridge, was very happy when I saw her, for a letter had been received from her brother Douglas, saying all was well with him.

During October, it was reported that a series of proficiency tests was being arranged for Devon land girls. Recruits, among other things, were to be tested in general knowledge, milking, and driving and harnessing a horse and cart. There was a great need of women car drivers to conduct milk rounds for farmers who were both producers and retailers. As a result of the registration of women employed in retail shops, there was a steady flow of recruits entering the Women's Land Army, many of them from Exeter.

The *Western Times* of Friday 31 October featured an appeal for books after Plymouth's library was destroyed in the blitz. Mr F.C. Cole, the Plymouth City Librarian, stated that 'Plymouth City Library had a stock of 93,000 books. Then came the blitz. The central library and one of its branches were destroyed. So were 72,000 books and all records and catalogues. What a holocaust and what an end to the work of building and extending collections over a period of 65 years.'

Mr Cole made the statement at an Exeter Rotary Club's lunch where he appealed for help. 'Plymouth,' he said, 'could not make good the loss in a reasonable period out of its own resources.'

The US Navy shore patrol in Plymouth outside their headquarters at St George's Hall, East Street, Stonehouse in Plymouth. The Navy Police were remembered for their smartness and patrolled the city, sorting out any trouble that occurred with service personnel.

An appeal was launched through the medium of the Ministry of Information's regional committees and the publication of a letter signed by West Country authors. About 900 volumes had reached Mr Cole directly. Many public libraries were receiving books on behalf of Plymouth and offers continued to come in from all parts of the United Kingdom. He estimated that, as the result of the return of books on issue at the time of the blitz, those salvaged, and from offers received, there would be about 24,000 volumes available. That would mean that 48,000 more would be required to reach the peace-time total.

Towards the end of October part-time members of thirteen fire brigades in Devon, with messengers, dispatch riders and girl telephonists, attended a weekend camp at Starcross. The first to be held in the county, the event was an unqualified success. Extensive drills were carried out and a feature was the response to a test call during the night. Among the visitors, were the Mayor of Exeter (Mr R. Glave Saunders) and the Sheriff (Mr E.J. Mansfield).

Rest cures and baths for blitz heroes

At the beginning of November an appeal was issued for rest cottages in Devon for blitz workers. It was stated that Civil Defence men and women from Plymouth, Bristol and London had already been given holidays in several parts of the country and had been welcomed as guests in Devon houses.

The Devon Committee which ran the scheme for providing short 'rest cures' for blitz heroes, wanted to extend its work, to find houses and cottages, which owners would lend for parties of wardens, firemen, and women air raid workers. The scheme was run by the War Organization of the British Red Cross Society and the Order of St John.

The *Western Morning News* of Wednesday 12 November carried an article about free baths. The Lifebuoy Emergency Bath Unit offered by Lever Brothers Ltd, of Port Sunlight, for the use of Plymouth and district, commenced operations on 11 November. The Lord Mayor formally received the bath at Victoria Road School in St Budeaux. The object of the service was to provide people living in badly blitzed districts with hot shower baths and hot water. After a bad blitz, it was be taken where it was needed most, giving priority to rest centres and civil defence personnel and districts where gas and water supplies were temporarily suspended. During non-blitzed periods it was to work to a set programme, which included a number of appointments with local schools.

The unit was self-contained and comprised a large van containing an oil-fired water heater, capable of heating to bath temperature, four and a half gallons of water per minute, eight dressing rooms and shower cubicles complete with towels, soap, scrubbing brushes and bathing caps, all of which were provided free. A reserve supply of water was also carried, which enabled operations to proceed when the general water supply had been cut off. The unit was one of a large fleet which was to service blitzed areas throughout the country. In Plymouth, posters were to be displayed in areas where the unit was to operate, giving details of the times and sites. The service was free and everyone was welcome. The unit was presented by Mr J. Hamilton, on behalf of the chairman and board of directors of Lever Brothers Ltd. Eight schoolboys were the first to use the bath.

In November, the Lord Mayor of Bristol, who had been visiting South Devon, spoke of his meeting with evacuees from the city during the week. He told *The Western Morning News*:

My general impression, which is corroborated by those who went with me, is that our Bristol children are being efficiently and kindly cared for. Without exception, they all seemed very happy indeed. I asked a number of them whether they had put on weight, and some said from 6lb to 10lb and one, over a stone! They are bright and cheerful and in excellent spirits. We went into many of the little Devon homes, where our youngsters are staying, and found them spotlessly clean, comfortable, and homely. The foster parents have taken the children into their family circles as their own. I impressed upon the children the importance of remaining away from Bristol for the present. The civic leaders of the chief towns, the county authorities, clergy, school managers, members of the various local Councils, in fact, the community generally, are taking a live interest in the welfare of our children.

It was most gratifying to learn that the standard of the physique of our children and the excellence of their clothing and equipment created a profound impression when they reached Devon.

During November, Mr G.C. Hayter-Hames, the chairman of Devon War Agricultural Committee, emphasised the importance of the potato crop in an address to members of the Moretonhampstead Farmers' Union at Chagford. He said that in pre-war days, Devon grew about 6,000 acres of potatoes. In the previous year, this was about 12,000 acres but in 1941, it was 25,000 acres and their quota for 1942 was 32,000 acres.

Labour was a limiting factor, but in this they needed more co-operation. The Agricultural Committee asked farmers to let them know early if they required help to lift their crops. He said that in the previous year, practically nobody had answered the call, and this year there were so few that the committee were at one time against making any gang labour available.

In the course of the discussion, Mr E. Andrews congratulated the War Agricultural Committee on the excellence of the female labour that had been going around the country potato picking.

On 21 November a single German bomber flew over Plymouth but it was met with such resistance from an intensified barrage that it flew eastwards and dropped its bombs at Ugborough. A bungalow was hit, killing one of its occupants, an evacuee from Plymouth. Eight other people were injured.

The *Western Morning News* of Saturday 22 November carried a story about children helping those affected by the blitz. Children of South Australia had made a touching gesture to children in Britain's heavily blitzed towns. They had formed a Patriotic School Fund and had sent a cheque for £1,000, 'especially for Christmas' to Sir Charles McCann, the Agent General for South Australia in London. Sir Charles said, 'I was deeply touched by the kindly thought behind this gift. As a result of it children in Plymouth, Hull, Liverpool, Southampton, Portsmouth, Bermondsey and East London will be taken to parties and pantomimes, or given toys and additional Christmas fare. I have asked the clergy in each area, who are in close touch with these children to help with the distribution. The gift is truly seasonal and I am happy to be able to help bring additional brightness to those children who have suffered so much.'

On 24 November 1941, a Polish fighter brought down a German plane over Plymouth. The four crew members successfully baled out. One of them, who was wounded, was pushed out over Plympton while the others were taken prisoner near Bickleigh. The plane crashed at Roborough and the wreckage spread over two fields.

At the beginning of December, it was reported that Devon was ahead of Cornwall and Somerset in the County Warships Weeks Championship, but had fallen from ninth to twelfth position in the table.

Weeks at Teignmouth, Ilfracombe, and Lynton had raised a total of £301.580, or £8 1s 9d per head of the population, which was 4s 4d below the average the previous week.

Cornwall, which was unrepresented in the weekly table, occupied 16th position. Warships Weeks in the Truro and Fowey areas had raised £254,013 or an average of £6 19s 3d.

The *Western Morning News* of Thursday 4 December carried a story under the headline NAZI PLANE ON SOUTH WEST DROME. It was reported that a German plane landed on an RAF aerodrome in the South West. An RAF plane had just landed,

A downed German plane. The plane crashed near to Roborough and the wreckage spread out over two fields.

when it was followed on to the illuminated runway by the German machine, which made a good landing. There was no information as to whether the German airmen intended giving themselves up, landed at the aerodrome in error, or had hostile intent. During the night, German planes flew over South Wales, after flying over the South West. The enemy plane was understood to be a bomber and was intact.

It was also reported that a German airman, who mistook the Bristol Channel for the English Channel, had landed on a British aerodrome and was immediately taken prisoner. Visibility was bad as the German flew round over the west coast, waiting for an opportunity to attack shipping. The pilot lost his bearings and, after wandering round for hours with his petrol running short, decided to head for home. However, he made a mistake, evidently thinking he was safely over France when he saw an aerodrome where lights were burning and planes landing. He brought his machine down and was followed across the aerodrome by British armoured vehicles. When the pilot reached the other side of the runway, the aerodrome defence personnel surrounded him with tommy-guns and took him prisoner.

Night fighters were heard in combat with raiders in south-west England on the previous Tuesday night. Two enemy aircraft were destroyed and fell into the sea; there were no survivors. Berlin reported that the Luftwaffe had bombed harbour works at a port on the English south-west coast. Inhabitants in the area said that enemy planes had tried repeatedly to reach objectives on the coast but were driven off. One of the enemy planes was caught by a British fighter and townspeople heard its cannon fire and the crackle of machine guns. Similar treatment was dealt out to the other raider.

America enters the war

On 7 December, Japan attacked Pearl Harbor and declared war on America. This had a direct affect on the people of Devon. Four days later, Germany and Italy also declared war on America. Americans were drafted in the services and were told that they could be sent anywhere in the world. President Roosevelt met with Winston Churchill in Washington and it was agreed that contingents of American troops would start arriving in the UK, mainly in the West Country, in January 1942.

Christmas Day saw more shortages than in previous years. However, in Torquay, 400 French and Belgian children were entertained and treated to whatever was available. People with enough ration coupons were able to buy sweets and chocolate, which were well stocked in shops. Many stores reported a brisk trade in present buying for loved ones.

Soon after Pearl Harbor, the British battleship HMS *Prince of Wales* and the battlecruiser HMS *Repulse* were sunk by Japanese torpedo bombers off the coast of Malaya. On Christmas Eve, David William John Llewellyn Loving, aged 29, of Maiden House, Exeter Road, Exmouth, was reported killed in action on the *Repulse*. He was an electrical artificer and left a wife and two children.

Mr and Mrs G. Perry, of 10, Albion Street, Exmouth, received news that their son, Norman, was missing. He was also on the *Repulse*, and would have been 18 on the day after the ship went down. His friend, Peter Anstey (17), the son of Mr and Mrs R. Anstey, of Elston Cottage, Budleigh Salterton, was also reported missing from the same ship. A friend of Perry, Leonard Mewse (18), son of Mr and Mrs E. Mewse, of 8, Woodville Road, Exmouth, a telegraphist on the *Prince of Wales* , was another reported missing. Among the survivors from the battleship was William Skinner, whose parents resided in Rosebery Road, Exmouth.

The *Western Morning News* of Saturday 27 December reported that Christmas was quiet in Torquay, the quietest Torbay district had known for many years. Hotels and boarding houses were comfortably full but there was nothing approaching the rush experienced of the previous year and accommodation was more than equal to the demand. There was a surprisingly large audience at a concert of seasonable music in Torquay Pavilion by the Municipal Orchestra, under Mr E.W. Goss, on the afternoon of Christmas Day. On Christmas Eve, 400 children in the Belgian and French Colony in the South West were entertained to tea.

Dartmouth had a quiet Christmas. Men engaged in industry returned to work on Boxing Day. Dartmouth Young Fellowship sang carols in the streets over the Christmas season. The victory sign was prominent in decorations at the North Devon Infirmary, Barnstaple, where the staff contributed to the enjoyment of the patients. At the Public Assistance Institute, Barnstaple, the special Christmas fare included beer and minerals, while the children of the cottage homes had a special treat, for turkey figured on their menu. The Salvation Army Band and girl singers entertained and a new and appreciated feature was the showing of a Ministry of Information film.

Generally, in North Devon, it was a quiet stay-at-home Christmas and travel was limited.

It was reported towards the end of December that Flight Officer Paul Temple Cotton, of the Royal Air Force Volunteer Reserve, 208 Squadron, whose home was in Branscombe, East Devon, had been awarded the Distinguished Flying Cross for gallantry displayed in operations against the enemy. The announcement of the award stated:

> One day in November 1941 this officer carried out an extremely important reconnaissance. During the flight, his aircraft was attacked by two Messerschmitt 109s, but Flight Officer Cotton drove them off and flew on to complete his task. His skill, coolness, and courage enabled him to obtain information of vital importance.

Born in 1913, Flight Officer Cotton was educated at Wellington and Cambridge. He was a member of the University Air Squadron. He joined the King's African Rifles Reserve of Officers in 1938 and in June 1940 was commissioned in the RAF.

The *Western Morning News* of Wednesday 31 December carried a New Year message from Mr Leslie Hore-Belisha, the MP for Devonport:

> During the past year Devonport has borne its full share in sustaining the cause for which we are fighting. The three towns have taken heavy blows with West Country courage. A great strain has been placed on the civic authorities, civil defence workers and the police. The business community and private citizens have undergone exacting trials. The most glorious traditions have been upheld by men in Devonport ships of the Royal Navy, and by Devonport men in the Army, the RAF, and the Merchant Navy. Some of them, in circumstances of great heroism, have paid the supreme forfeit. May their relatives be comforted. 1942 offers us another challenge. The new year cannot be an easy one. In comradeship and in determination we will face it unitedly, with unshakable confidence in the final issue of the struggle. My thoughts are with my constituents wherever they may be. I wish them and theirs success in all their endeavours.

At the end of December, North Devon faced a beer shortage owing partly to the heavy demand over the Christmas period. One Barnstaple licensed house posted the notice: 'No beer until Thursday'.

CHAPTER 4

1942 – Run Rabbit Run

At the beginning of January, cases were heard at Tavistock police court against defendants who had bought or sold rabbits in excess of the maximum prices allowed under the Rabbits Order of 1941. It was said that the cases had a serious effect on food and stopped the fair supply of rabbit to the county. All defendants were fined and the worst offender had to pay £4 to the court.

In January, Plymouth's salvage campaign for scrap metal continued and householders were asked to give up their gates and fences as well as any other metal they could spare. The Women's Voluntary Service was responsible for organising salvage drives which included the removal of railings. They also collected aluminium pots and pans, jelly moulds, kettles, paper and rubber and even artificial limbs. Much of this was never re-used but the drives brought together people and raised morale.

The *Western Morning News* of Wednesday 21 January carried a story under the headline MANY GIFTS TO PLYMOTHIANS. The generosity of Americans to Plymouth was probably not fully realised by most people in the city and much of it was entirely due to the fact that Plymouth's Lady Mayoress and MP was a native of Virginia. Daily, since the blitz on Plymouth the previous spring, crates had arrived at Elliot Terrace, on the Hoe, addressed to Lady Astor personally and crammed with gifts of clothing and toys from people and organisations in various parts of Canada and the United States. Several rooms in the house were full of the gifts, although a large quantity had been given into the care of the Salvation Army and the Orthopaedic and Prince of Wales's Hospitals. So valuable were the contents of the remaining crates that Mrs W.J.W. Modley, deputy Lady

A girl with collected milk bottle tops. Anything that could be salvaged was salvaged and milk bottle tops were collected for their aluminium to make Lancaster bombers.

Mayoress, told a representative of the *Western Morning News* that she had made arrangements for their insurance.

It was difficult for those who had not seen the crates unpacked to realise the love and sympathy which had prompted the donors and those who had packed the gifts. Lovely toys and Christmas stockings (some arrived a little late for Christmas, but nevertheless brought joy to the children who were to have them) were wrapped up in garments to ensure their safe transit. Exquisitely knitted baby clothes were carefully sorted and kindly thought was revealed in the inclusion of mittens, socks, and bonnets chosen to match the other garments. Suits, shirts, under clothing and nightwear for men, women's clothing, boots and shoes, cosy knitted quilts, down quilts and blankets were among the huge supplies which had flowed in a continuous stream to Lady Astor for the relief of victims of the war.

Many organisations in both America and Canada had repeatedly sent gifts and from some towns had come gifts from a number of different people and organizations. In Toronto, they had formed an Astor Club and from this club many gifts had come to Elliot Terrace. Money had also been sent and often a cheque to pay freightage accompanied a crate. Much of the clothing and bedding was new and of excellent quality and the worn clothing was all in good condition. Twice a week, Mrs Modley and helpers were busy at Elliot Terrace unpacking, sorting and dispatching the garments and toys. The use of Lord Astor's house had been further extended, for in addition to the downstairs flat being given over to the use of service women as a club, he had now given a flat on the first floor.

Towards the end of January, Plymouth Corporation invited tenders for the removal of Plymouth Pier which had been severely damaged by enemy action.

The Luftwaffe continued their attacks on Devon during the second week of February when planes appeared above Torquay and Exmouth, where houses were destroyed and several people were killed.

During February, Company Sergeant Major R.R. Lee, of the Barnstaple Home Guard, was the first member of his battalion to receive the recently created Certificate of Merit for good service.

Sir Stafford Cripps announced to the House of Commons in February that extravagance was a thing of the past and there should be no petrol used for pleasure driving. He also said there would be a cut in clothing rations and sporting events should be curtailed. Silk stockings were no longer available and many women coloured their legs with gravy browning to give the desired effect.

On Tuesday 10 February, Plymouth City Council promised to restore the memorial gates at Hartley Park after the war. The gates had been torn down as scrap for the war effort. Alderman S. Stephens moved a notice of motion asking that they be restored to their previous state and position. The gates had previously been presented to the city by the late Mr Ambrose Andrews, a former mayor of the city. Their purpose was to safeguard children playing in the park from road traffic. Alderman Stephens said, 'You can imagine the feelings of the widow when she looked out one morning recently to see the gates being torn down. Nobody seemed to have assumed any direct responsibility for it. The value of the gates to the war effort is infinitesimal but their sentimental value is very great.'

The *Western Times* of Friday 13 February carried the story of an early morning raid. At least five people were killed during the enemy raid over a south-west coastal town early in the morning. The dead included three sisters who lived in the same house and a number of people were injured. Houses were demolished and two churches extensively damaged. In one of the houses, near those demolished, there were four elderly people, together with a woman and a baby, who had been previously bombed out of Plymouth. Another woman in the same house was bombed out from London eighteen months previously.

At the bottom of the same road, the occupier of a house which had its windows smashed, celebrated his 88th birthday the day before the attack. His only comment was, 'This is a birthday present I did not expect, still, it might have been worse.' The house next door had its front windows smashed but protective wire netting prevented glass from entering the rooms. The enemy planes were met with a fierce barrage and machine-gunned the streets as they swept over the town. ARP and civil defence services were soon in action attending the injured and clearing the debris. Bombs fell near a village further inland and dropped in a market garden doing little damage. An enemy raider was reported to have been brought down nearby. Raiders also visited another south-west town and dropped bombs, as a result of which one man was killed and four injured as well as some damage caused to property.

From Monday 16 February funds were raised at Sidmouth as part of their Warship Week. The town hoped to raise £120,000 and, by doing so, adopt HMS *Sidmouth*. A plaque was to be placed on the vessel, along with the town's civic badge, to celebrate the achievement. To raise the money, there had been military and civic parades, exhibitions, concerts, competitions, football matches, dances, whist drives and a host of other attractions. The town wholeheartedly supported the event and shopkeepers made up special displays to promote the event. By the following Thursday, almost £70,000 had been raised.

On Friday 20 February it was announced that Devonshire farmers had raised £1,500 for the Red Cross Agricultural Fund.

Towards the end of February, a Chagford officer was reported missing in action to his wife. Sub-Lieutenant C.R. Wood of the Fleet Air Arm was the pilot of the third plane of six Swordfish which made an attack on German battleships in the Channel. Sub-Lieutenant Wood was aged 26 and had married during the previous April.

On Monday 2 March Mrs Mary Fey, of the Seacroft Hotel, Teignmouth, was fined three guineas, including costs, by Teignmouth magistrates for obtaining rationed goods without giving up the necessary coupons.

On Tuesday 3 March it was announced that Bideford and district had raised £273,494 5s during Warship Week which far exceeded expectations.

The *Western Morning News* of Saturday 14 March carried a letter from Mr G.W. Copeland, of 25 Carfrae Terrace, Mount Gould, Plymouth who wrote about the indiscriminate taking of metal items:

The disappearance of the 17th century ducking stool, and possibly the Armada Cannon, from the ruins of the Athenaeum amounts to nothing less than looting, which the general order for the collection of scrap metal appears to have sanctioned and legalised. Collectors in their ignorance of what may still be of value in other respects naturally become over zealous, and therefore their activities should not only be controlled, but they should also be under some expert surveillance, when buildings (which may be, after all , still 'private') are being ransacked and rifled for what they might yield. If it be necessary to be so indiscriminate in the collection of scrap metal, which is not always 'scrap,' surely anything which can be shown to have historic or even intrinsic value that the enemy has left us should be granted a reprieve and treated with a certain amount of respect.

The ducking stool, it is true, did not look very prepossessing to the uninitiated after its ordeal by fire, but it was still capable of being repaired. It may interest those who do not already know of it that the bells of Charles Church are in process of removal. Two of the original peal still remain perched precariously in the tower, and those which fell are either shattered or badly cracked. One of them, however, still retains its outline intact, and as it is one of the oldest (it is dated 1782) it might very well be prescrved as a memento of what used to be. I strongly urge all lovers of Charles Church to try to do what they can to retain this bell.

On Saturday 28 March, it was announced that Exeter had the highest number of recruited cadets with five companies comprising of 370 members. Plymouth was the next highest with the enrolment of 250 cadets. All over Devon, 2,500 boys had joined since the formation of the ATC during the previous November.

At the end of March, it was reported that Exeter had raised £1,054,000 during Warship Week which was more than double the expected amount. The announcement was made from the balcony of the Guildhall, where the mayor and mayoress led the cheers as the total was disclosed.

Mr Vincent Thompson (chairman of the War Savings Committee) said, 'I think the city has made a contribution to the cause worthy of her traditions of unswerving faith in what this country and her allies stand for in this tremendous struggle.'

Nearby, Plymouth managed to raise an incredible £1,396, 493 ahead of Portsmouth, who had been in the lead, with a total of £1,229,906.

During April it was reported that Miss Johnson, a 65-year-old evacuee from London, had spent four days and nights in the open on Dartmoor having wandered from South Brent where she was billeted with Mr and Mrs E. Catt of 3 Nelson Terrace.

Miss Johnson left the house to take a walk but lost her bearings and wandered for hours while trying to find her way back. Without food, she grew weaker and weaker and, when rescued, was unable to say who she was or what had happened. She was found by the Dartmoor Hunt near to Warren Cross by Mr A. Piper, the whip of the hunt who gave her a pasty. Dr Creasy, of South Brent, gave her some milk from a hip flask before she was removed to South Brent on a stretcher.

On 12 April Charles Butler, steward of Bideford's Working Men's Conservative Association Club, was fined one guinea by Bideford borough magistrates in respect of a black-out offence. PC W.H.T. Bird stated that the defendant told him that the lights must have accidentally been switched on while the room was being cleaned and dusted. For a similar offence, Ann Mary Colwill, of 4 Wellbrook Terrace, Bideford, was fined 30s.

On 13 April tragedy struck when a Wellington Bomber crashed into the cliffs at Windbury near Hartland due to thick fog.

Mrs Jean Know, the commandant of the ATS pictured with Lady Astor at Plymouth on Thursday 16 April 1942. She later visited centres in Devon to confer with junior officers.

Zoos stayed open during the war and here a man and his daughter can be seen feeding a zebra at Paignton Zoo in April 1942.

Exeter bombed

The *Western Morning News* of Monday 27 April carried a story under the headline, HIGH DEATH TOLL. The story stated that a south-west town had experienced its most severe raid of the war in the early hours of the previous Saturday morning. High explosives and incendiary bombs were dropped in various parts of the town, causing a fairly high death toll and extensive damage. Several fires were caused; others were prevented through the pluck of young men and women, who tackled incendiaries with sandbags, stirrup pumps, earth and even their steel helmets. Several were clad only in their night attire, over which they had thrown greatcoats. They also did good work in removing furniture from a number of houses at which fires had been started. Members of the fire service worked heroically but they could not prevent several houses being gutted.

In a number of instances, there were direct hits on dwelling houses and the occupants were either killed outright or buried beneath the debris. Rescue parties were engaged until a late hour removing bodies from the wreckage. It was the second successive night on which the city had been attacked and it was one of the heaviest raids experienced. The death toll was feared to be heavy and many were injured, the majority not seriously. The raid developed late; it was entirely indiscriminate and directed against the civilian population. Dropping of flares, which illuminated the greater part of the town, was followed by incendiary and high explosive bombs in many parts of the city. The destruction although widespread, was not so severe as it might have been having regard to the nature of the attack. Four fire watchers were among the dead. It was the second time that the Fire Guard Service had suffered casualties. The party was on duty at a furniture repository and were standing in the street on the look-out for incendiaries when a high explosive crashed to earth nearby. Several houses in the street were demolished and the party was wiped out.

Bombs also fell in a residential district, where nine occupants of a teachers' hostel were killed. Several of the bombs failed to explode and the areas in which they fell were roped off and evacuated. Bomb disposal squads were in action later in the day.

Although newspapers were sworn to secrecy over the exact location of major bombing raids in the region, it was revealed a few days later that the 'south-west town' was in fact Exeter.

On 4 May twenty German bombers once again devastated the town centre of Exeter. The raid lasted seventy minutes. Thirty acres of the city were destroyed and 156 people were killed with a further 583 injured. Altogether, 1,500 houses were obliterated and 2,700 badly damaged. The Germans gloated about the devastation. One of the pilots was quoted in the *Western Morning News* as saying: 'We were glad when we saw our bombs fall on Exeter as we were conscious of the fact that we were fulfilling the Fuhrer's promise to retaliate blow for blow for the British attacks on German towns.'

On Friday 8 May civic and church leaders gathered with those bereaved to pay tribute to the people of Exeter who lost their lives on 4 May. Spring flowers were carried by the mourners to the ceremony at Higher Cemetery.

In the second week of May, King George VI and Queen Elizabeth visited the Royal Naval College at Dartmouth. They arrived at Kingswear by special train before taking a motor launch over the River Dart. Their visit had been a well-kept secret and it was only a few hours before their arrival that the news was leaked out. Flags began to appear everywhere and schoolchildren assembled along the embankment, also waving flags, on the route to the college.

The *Western Morning News* of Saturday 9 May told of the King and Queen's visit to the West Country. It reported that their majesties had forged another link of warm affection with the West Country. In a three-day programme touring Devon and Cornwall, which was brought to a close when the Royal train steamed out of the war-scarred city of Exeter, they made many intimate contacts with the war effort in its varied aspects.

Against the grim background of the West Country's mighty war effort and the blitz scars of Plymouth, there were many pleasant interludes which left a lingering memory, not only with the King and Queen, but also with the thousands who so heartily cheered them on their royal tour. When the Queen visited WRNS establishments, history mingled with the hard training of war. Her Majesty, the first English Queen to do so, made a voyage in a vessel manned entirely by women. For the most part,

The King and Queen visited the West Country during May 1942. The King toured the dockyard in Plymouth and inspected the RAF at Mount Wise and saw over 5,000 officers and ratings paraded at the Royal Naval Barracks.

the visit of the King and Queen was, for obvious reasons, a well-guarded secret. There were whisperings and rumours of the visit of 'important personages' but it was a pleasant surprise when the general public heard through police loud speakers an hour or two before that the King and Queen were coming. The news spread like wildfire. The result was a spontaneous turning out of the populations in every city, town and hamlet through which the procession passed. The King and Queen spent all Thursday afternoon in Plymouth, His Majesty visiting the Dockyard and making a tour of some of the workshops and depot ships. The King also inspected the RAF at Mount Wise and saw over 5,000 officers and ratings paraded at the Royal Naval Barracks. There was also an inspection at the Royal Marine Barracks.

An announcement in the *Western Times* of Friday 5 June stated: 'Exeter has had a supply of oranges during the past week.'

Progress in the campaign to establish Girls' Training Corps Units in Devon continued in Exeter during June. There was a well-attended course at the Bishop Blackall School.

Dawlish sent £99 for the Church of England Waifs and Strays' Society. Of this sum, £69 was obtained by a 'Time and Talents' scheme. Meanwhile, a whist drive at Totnes raised £22 for the Mayor of Exeter's Air Raid Distress Fund.

The *Western Morning News* of Tuesday 9 June carried a report about a bomber which had been shot down. Shortly before dusk on Sunday 7 June, an RAF fighter shot down an enemy bomber into the sea off the south-west coast. The casualty list for the raid was heavier than anticipated. There were five dead and seven seriously injured. Swooping to within a few feet of the house tops, a tip and run force of German bombers dropped a small number of high explosive bombs. The attack was carried out in broad daylight. Visitors afterwards resumed their deck chairs, dinner at the hotels proceeded almost uninterruptedly, and within a few moments the even tenor of life proceeded. Civil Defence services, however, turned out promptly to deal with the resulting incidents. One bomb fell at the back of an amusement arcade. Slight damage was caused by the blast, and a few customers at a cafe were cut by flying glass. A number of shop windows in the vicinity were also broken and a row of cottages received a direct hit. The manager of a butcher's shop was sitting in his front room at the time. He was injured and taken to hospital as was his son. A block of flats was also demolished but almost all of the residents were out, two people were, however, injured and taken to hospital. Two elderly men, cousins, who were believed to be buried in the wreckage, walked up as rescue workers were searching for them. They had been to church and until they reached the corner of the road were unaware of their narrow escape.

During the beginning of June, a mobile gas van toured Plymouth so that people could test their respirators.

On Monday 21 June, at a special sitting of Tiverton County Bench, James Kilby, a 17-year-old soldier, was brought up in custody charged with having, at Thorverton on 21 June, shot at PC Leonard Walter Minter at Silverton with intent to murder. Superintendent Johnson said that late on the previous evening, a straw rick was found to be on fire on the Cadbury–Thorverton Road and PC Minter was detailed to make inquiries. He arrived on the scene at 11.35pm and saw the accused and questioned him about the fire. The accused

Two evacuee children enjoy pasties given to them for their journey before they're billeted in Cornwall. They are pictured waiting for a train at North Road Station in Plymouth. They were accompanied by 40 other children.

was in uniform, with equipment, and in possession of a service rifle. PC Minter told him to put down the rifle while he went to get his bicycle. The accused threatened to shoot PC Minter if he approached. The officer advanced and the soldier put the rifle to his shoulder and fired. PC Minter was injured in the thigh and legs and had to be taken to the Royal Devon and Exeter Hospital. Kilby was arrested and remanded in custody while he awaited trial. The charge was later commuted to causing grievous bodily harm for which Kilby was sentenced to three years in Borstal.

On Friday 26 June it was reported that the 12-ton cast-iron anvil block of a 40-ton steam hammer, used for heavy smithy work in the last century, had been contributed by Mr H. Morris, of Morris Brothers, to Tavistock Scrap Metal Week.

Towards the end of June, the joint Red Cross and St John Ambulance flag day at Exmouth raised £263.

During July, many organisations raised money for the Exeter Air Raid Relief Fund. The Farmers' Union raised £820 while the Teignmouth Licensed Victuallers association held a dance which raised £80.

The *Western Morning News* of Friday 3 July reported on air raids in the South West. Four enemy bombers were destroyed by RAF fighters on the night of 1 July, three over enemy territory and one over Britain. Bombs and incendiaries fell at various points on the south and west coast of England but no concentrated attack developed.

Members of a barrage balloon crew remove the bandstand on Plymouth Hoe taking anything that can be saved for the scrap metal drive.

German raiders dropped high explosives at the junction of two streets. Four lives were lost and a number of people injured. A good deal of private property was either destroyed or damaged. One of the victims was a young sailor named Smith who had recently been the recipient of an award for gallantry at sea and was at home on leave. Local rescue and ambulance services put in several hours of good work. An inland town was subjected to some machine gunning and bullet holes were made in a roof in one district. No casualties were caused when two south-west coastal towns were also machine gunned during the early hours of the previous morning.

On Monday 6 July William Harman, aged 41 and a skilled labourer living at Phoenix Street, Plymouth, pleaded guilty to walking out of Devonport Dockyard with five gills of petrol worth 3d. In court it was stated that the petrol was either stolen or unlawfully obtained without the use of a valid coupon. Harman said that he was taking the petrol home for cleaning purposes. He had no motor bike and his car was laid up. His job was very dirty and his clothes became oily and he used the petrol to clean up. The court heard that he had an unblemished record of 22 years' service. His solicitor asked the court to be lenient and hoped that he would be able to retain his job. The chairman of the court fined him £1 saying: 'We are impressed with your record and do not want to do you any serious injury.'

Frank Dymond, of 19 Silver Street, Bideford, appeared in court during the beginning of July. He was a member of the Bideford Home Guard and thought that he was 'doing something for the benefit of his country' by practising target shooting with an air rifle on top of Bideford Cinema. In court he was charged with carrying and using a rifle without a licence. Charles William Turner, of 2 Rushmead, Fremington, with whom he was practising, was similarly charged.

Inspector Rendell stated that the defendants admitted using the gun to practise target shooting and told PC Hutchings that they were unaware that a licence was needed. The case against Dymond was dismissed as was the case against Turner under the Probation of Offenders Act on payment of costs.

Torquay attacked

During the Bank Holiday of Monday 4 August, bombs were dropped on 'a south-west coastal town' later named as Torquay.

The *Western Morning News* reported that the attack occurred at lunchtime. Swooping from the clouds, a small force of raiders sprayed the beaches and shopping streets with machine-gun fire and deadly cannon shells. Fortunately, most of the visitors were indoors at the time or casualties would have proved heavy. Four people, some of them women, were known to have been killed when direct hits were scored on terraced residential houses.

A preparatory school for girls, which had broken up for the summer holidays ten days before, was completely demolished. The dining hall, where in term time about thirty girls and teachers would have been seated at lunch, was a total wreck. The building was locked up and completely empty at the time and no casualties resulted from the incident. The house of a sector warden, which adjoined the school, was damaged but the occupants were unhurt.

Three of the fatal casualties occurred in a row of dwellings which received a direct hit. An ice-cream store on the opposite side of the road was wrecked by the blast.

In August, it was announced that Alexandra Rose Day in Plymouth had been the most successful since the event's inauguration. A cheque for £1,305 was presented to Plymouth hospitals by Mrs R. Wagner, the chairman of the committee. Mr W.J. Law, the honorary secretary of the hospital, said that the cheque spoke of the kindness of the people of Plymouth in helping to keep the hospitals going.

On Thursday 6 August Robert Perry was sentenced to 12 months' hard labour at Crediton for posing as a squadron leader, an ATC executive and a flight lieutenant. He had faced two charges of obtaining food, drink and money and a third charge of having stated that he was a resident engineer in the RAF. The accused stated that he used the titles out of 'swank,' and also to impress people. The court heard that he had been convicted of eleven other such offences since 1928.

Trooper Jetley, from Ilfracombe, talks to his family back home, from the desert in Africa. He is seen relaying his message using a mobile recording van during August 1942.

The *Western Morning News* of Friday 7 August carried a story about an American abroad. It stated that an American soldier had lost his wallet at Ilfracombe. For over two days, it lay on a hill. Hundreds of holidaymakers must have passed over it. Eventually, it was found by Mrs Minnie Morgan of Kenley, Surrey, who handed it to

Boys of the Devon Army Cadet Force receiving training during August 1942. The boys were aged between 14 and 17 years old and studied map reading and field strategy as well as learning how to use the army's up to date instruments and weaponry. At 17, they were drafted into the Home Guard before later joining the regular army.

the police. The soldier was given back his wallet and the £72 it contained. 'You British are sure mighty honest,' was his comment as he rewarded Mrs Morgan with £12. He also gave a donation to the police orphanage.

On Friday 14 August, Barnstaple Rural Council applied for deferment from calling-up, under the Armed Forces Act, of their sanitary engineer Mr S.P. Smith.

During August, Totnes Council for British-Soviet Unity handed over a cheque for £10 to the mayor for Mrs Churchill's Aid-to-Russia Fund as a result of a dance.

On Friday 21 August it was announced that Dawlish had raised £28 1s for the Church of England Waifs and Strays through a flag day organised by Mrs Prince.

On Sunday 30 August the anti-gas school at Newton Abbot was the scene of a local stirrup-pump competition organised by the fire prevention office. The winners were the Newton Abbot Hospital team who won a £2 savings certificate for each member of the group.

Towards the end of August, Mrs Mackenny, of Ermington, was informed that her son, LSBA Mackenny, was a prisoner of war in Japanese hands.

Captain the Hon. Erskine A. Nicolson DSO, a member of Tavistock Rural Council, was informed that his youngest son, 20-year-old Sub-Lieutenant Peter Trevelyan Nicolson DSC, of the Royal Naval Reserve, had been killed in action. He was in the

Dunkirk Channel in command of a motor torpedo boat waiting to pounce on a German convoy when, after firing two torpedoes which sank an enemy vessel, he was hit by a shell splinter fired from a shore battery. He is buried in Sheepstor Churchyard.

The *Western Morning News* of Tuesday 1 September featured a story about a Torquay man's death. It told that a verdict of suicide was returned on Charles Maryan, a painter, aged 50, of 99 Teignmouth Road, Torquay. He took his own life while suffering from acute depression and was found with severe throat lacerations in an air-raid shelter. Mrs Maryan gave evidence that she and her husband had come to Torquay from Tunbridge Wells, where they had been in the thick of the Battle of Britain. The deceased had never recovered from the effects of the bombing and his depression heightened when he was sent to a town to do air-raid repairs.

Female service personnel using the control room map in Plymouth during the city's communication exercise during August 1942.

Maryan's workmate described how he found the deceased kneeling in an air-raid shelter in the garden of a house at which they were doing emergency repairs. He had throat wounds and was obviously dead.

The *Western Morning News* of Wednesday 2 September reported that housewives in Devon were unhappy with the quality of the new Welsh coal in use. It was said that it was unsuitable for cooking and required a lot of attention. A local merchant commented that they 'must grin and burn it'.

During September, a raid on Paignton killed thirteen people and 1,200 houses were damaged. Every woman in Paignton who was aged between 20 and 45 was required to register for fire watching duties.

On 18 September there was an air raid on Dartmouth. Bombs were dropped on the harbour and a lighter in the river was hit. Two bombs were also dropped on the Naval College. Two men were killed on the lighter and a WRNS was killed at the college.

With American troops stationed in many parts of Devon, many locals had their first contact with black soldiers. Racism was rife in many parts of the US. However, during September, the Chief Constable of Devon received instructions that the British Police were not to enforce any American order to 'prohibit certain places out of bounds to coloured troops'.

On 26 September, Richard Beaty, an American, crash landed his Spitfire IX BS148 in a field near Kingsbridge. He was badly injured but survived the incident.

A hundred fire fighters were welcomed to Plymouth on Tuesday 29 September where they paraded at Greenbank. The men were all volunteers who had left their Canadian homes to help the men of Britain make sure that their homes don't burn. Most of the men were trained firemen in their own country.

A fire at Lloyd's Bank, Bedford Street, Plymouth. Many of the major banks had their premises completely destroyed. These included Barclays in Princess Square, Lloyds and National Provisional in Bedford Street and the Midland in Bedford Street and Union Street.

Here, a building is hosed down to stop the fire spreading while others clear away bricks and rubble. The great heat generated from these fires could easily ignite adjacent premises. In August 1939, with war approaching, the Auxiliary Fire Service were issued with tin helmets and their red fire engines were repainted grey and all members were summoned to their stations.

Fire fighters hose down another bomb damaged building. Fire fighters resources were so stretched that many fires couldn't be reached and eventually just burnt themselves out. Here, fire fighters from Exeter help out in Plymouth. Fire fighters from all the surrounding districts were called upon to assist with the impossible task of quelling the fires.

During September 1942, Canadian firefighters arrived in Plymouth to aid the local division of the National Firefighting Service. They were inspected by the Deputy Lord Mayor (Alderman W.J.W. Modley) after a civic welcome.

Towards the end of September, it was announced that the DSO had been awarded to a Dawlish man, Major Dick Regnand Curzon Boileau, of the King's Royal Rifle Corps, for gallant and distinguished service in the Middle East.

Court reports and inquests

The *Western Morning News* of Tuesday 6 October, reported on a case of a home guard who did not attend parades. Private E.L. Bridle, of 38 New Street, Exmouth, was charged with absenting himself from duty as a member of the Home Guard during June and July. He pleaded guilty at court and was fined £2.

Inspector Abrahams said that the defendant joined as a Local Defence Volunteer in 1940 and then became a member of the Home Guard. The regulations necessitated his doing a certain amount of training. He was employed at a local cinema and, as it was difficult for him to do parades on weekdays, he was instructed to parade on Sundays. Since June, he had not attended a parade and had ignored letters written to him. He had treated the matter with contempt.

A woman in court shouted: 'He is only just 17.' The defendant said that he joined at first because he liked it. He was then 15 years of age but said he was 17.

The chairman, in announcing the decision of the bench, said he hoped the example would be a warning to others in their duty for the protection of the country.

Birching for older boys for certain offences was advocated by the justices at Devon Quarter Sessions on Wednesday 7 October. The court decided to make representations to the Secretary of State to raise the age limit for birching to 16 for all indictable offences including cruelty to animals, aggravated assault on a woman or child, false alarm of fire and malicious damage to property.

Sir George Robertson, chairman of the committee, submitted the recommendation, noting that acts of juvenile delinquency had risen by 41 per cent since the outbreak of war. Mr G.H.F. Kingdon said: 'It may not be altogether wise to send those naughty boys to approved school. Many of us think that what they deserve is a darned good spanking and we should like to see that carried out. They are not criminals but full of mischief.'

An inquest was resumed at Barnstable on Wednesday 14 October regarding the death of a young soldier. Robert William Jones, aged 20, died in the North Devon Infirmary of a gunshot wound while taking part in a gun demonstration where live ammunition was not supposed to be used.

A staff sergeant said that he examined the magazine used and passed it as correct. Superintendent Melhuish said that it looked like the only solution was that a live round had been left in the magazine. However, when it had been examined, it had been empty. A lance corporal in charge of stores said that it was not possible for the magazine to contain a live round.

A soldier who was taking part in the demonstration said that he was standing about a yard in front of the gun with the deceased standing behind him. The witness felt a shot penetrate his left arm and the deceased was hit in the stomach and fell to the ground. The coroner stated: 'I hope, whatever else may be the result of any inquiry which may have been held, a much more serious inspection will be ordered of these magazines.'

A verdict of misadventure' was recorded.

On Friday 23 October it was announced that Plymouth YMCA United Service Men's Institute in Union Street had raised £23 for Lady Astor's Aid to China Fund.

The youth of Plymouth were asked to assist the National ARP Animals Committee with the distribution of indestructible identity discs and animal owners were asked to place their names on a national animal register.

On Friday 30 October, it was announced that Captain Geoffrey Osmond, the well-known Sidmouth rugby forward, who was reported missing after the Dieppe raid, was, in fact, a prisoner of war.

Towards the end of October, Newton Abbot reported that it had raised £122,250 in the Tanks for Attack campaign.

The YMCA providing tea for the troops. The British YMCA played a big part in both world wars providing food, drink and writing materials from special YMCA huts. Their canteen was open 24 hours a day supplying meals to the armed forces.

At an inquest in Plymouth during the beginning of November, a verdict of accidental death was recorded on Ellen Ivey, aged 92, who died after falling while taking down a black-out curtain. She resided at Wilton Street.

Minehead magistrates imposed fines of £70 on Friday 6 November on businesses which were selling utility goods for higher than the permitted levels. In the case against Messrs Floyd and Sons of Minehead, an inspector from the Board of Trade found two women's overcoats priced at 98s and 6d each when the permitted price was 83s 10d. The firm pleaded guilty and it was stated that the clothes weren't clearly marked as utility wear. They were fined £25 with three guineas costs.

Minehead and District Co-operative Society was also fined £25 for selling men's pants at 6¼d and 7¼d above the permitted level, men's vests at 6¼d and women's vests at 4d and 3d, again above the correct level allowed. It was stated that the pricing had been done by an assistant who had calculated the purchase tax incorrectly.

Messrs Stroud Ltd were also fined for offering for sale a women's dress at 7¾d, again, above the maximum price allowed.

A story featured in the *Western Morning News* of Wednesday 11 November about the inquest into a young man's death. Eric John Taunton, aged 20, a cadet, was found shot through the head in a Sidmouth hotel lavatory on the previous Monday morning.

It was stated at his inquest that there was evidence that he was worried about a brother who was a prisoner of war and feared he would be put into chains.

The Coroner returned a verdict that death was due to a self-inflicted gunshot wound to the head while the balance of his mind was disturbed. He expressed sympathy with the parents.

The *Western Morning News* of Monday 16 November reported that Plymouth city police were working in close conjunction with the navy, army and the air force, as well as with the employment exchange, in a bid to crack down on people not carrying their ID cards. They were also trying to catch people who had been dodging their registration for military or national service.

On Saturday 14 November the police visited a popular cafe in Plymouth where about 100 people were having morning coffee. At the cafe, all the people they checked were civilians. About ten were unable to produce identity cards and were served with official notices to produce them within forty-eight hours at the police station.

At 9 o'clock the same night, they went in force to a well-known public house in Union Street. The doors were barred and about 300 people were inside drinking. Fewer than 100 civilians were present. When they were checked, 20 to 25 per cent of the civilians were unable to produce their identity cards. Those who were unable to satisfy National Service inquiries were subject to further investigation.

War Week in Plymouth, The aim of the campaign was to raise £1 million and their slogan was 'Turn Your Money into Victory'.

On Friday 27 November it was reported that Mr J. Wooland, for the local Food Control Committee, alleged in court that a Plymouth restaurant proprietor had made grossly exaggerated returns to the Food Office. The defendant, Antony Photiades, of the Imperial Restaurant in Union Street, was summoned for contravening the Rationing Order of 1942 and for failing to keep an accurate record of meals and hot beverages consumed and the quantity of each rationed food obtained and held by the establishment. Photiades was fined £25 and also had to pay three guineas in costs.

In the third week of December, the Admiralty informed the authorities in Plymouth that accommodation and berthing arrangements were required at Appledore for training purposes. Camps were set up in Falmouth, Fowey, Plymouth, Salcombe, Dartmouth and Teignmouth. The bases were used by the US 4th and 29th Infantry Divisions.

The story of the trial of a Barnstaple youth was carried in the *Western Morning News* of Tuesday 15 December. It mentioned that allegations of two attacks in the black-out, one on a man of 76 and the other on a young woman, were made by the police against Ivor Samuel Oliver Short, aged 17, of Arlington Beccott, who appeared before Barnstaple borough magistrates on remand.

Short was first charged that on 4 November, being armed with an offensive weapon, a stick, he feloniously robbed Albert Kiff and stole a silver watch and chain, various documents and 2s 6d in money to the total value of approximately £5.

Superintendent P. Melhuish said it was alleged at about 9pm on 4 November in Church Walk, just off High Street, Barnstaple, Mr Kiff was walking towards his home in Trinity Street when he was struck from behind. He collapsed and remained there all night until he was found and taken to hospital. Some of Mr Kiff's belongings were found in the possession of the accused.

When questioned, Short said, 'I didn't do it.' On being questioned about his movements on the night in question, he said, 'I knocked him on the head with a stick. I wanted some fish and chips.'

The accused also struck Ruth Spearman with a lead-weighted stick several times causing her to need stitches.

Short was committed for trial at Devon Assize, and remained in custody meanwhile. He had previous convictions and was later sent to Borstal for three years.

The *Western Morning News* of Friday 18 December reported on a children's Christmas party. About seventy children from the Channel Islands, most of them evacuees to Britain when their homes were overrun by the Germans, had a well-organised Christmas party at the Plymouth Swarthmore Settlement. This was due to the co-operation of the Channel Islands Society, the Plymouth Council of Social Service and the *Western Morning News'* Empty Stocking Fund.

The excitement of a film entertainment paved the way for tea, when the children had all the treats that the fourth wartime Christmas could provide. All eyes were on the huge Christmas tree, reaching from floor to ceiling, on which lights blazed and branches hung heavily with presents. In due course, Father Christmas made his distribution and each child, in addition to a present, received fruit and chocolate.

On Christmas Day a concert was held at the Royal Cinema in Plymouth in aid of the Prisoners of War Fund. Many well-known radio stars entertained. On Boxing Day, the Christmas pantomime, 'Aladdin', was presented at the Palace Theatre.

Members of the services who were away from home found a welcome awaiting them at the various YMCAs in Plymouth where turkey and Christmas pudding featured on the seasonal menu. Dinner was followed by concerts, competitions and entertainment of all kinds.

At Exeter Cathedral, community carol singing took place led by a military band. Most of the shattered windows had been boarded up and were replaced with small slotted windows.

The Mayor and Mayoress of Exeter distributed gifts to a large number of blitz children and spent the day visiting hospitals and children's homes.

CHAPTER 5

1943 – Over Here!

Kingsbridge was the first Devon town to experience bombing in 1943. A plan of mutual aid was put together in the event of further raids on Devon. Local authorities joined forces to procure prompt and complete action by giving assistance to any other authority within the area whose town had been damaged or distressed due to enemy bombing. The scheme also planned to loan resources wherever available. One collaboration of authorities united Plymouth, Okehampton, Kingsbridge, Salcombe, Tavistock and Broadwoodwidger.

On 10 January, seven FW190s flew low over Teignmouth dropping bombs on residential properties. People walking in the streets were gunned down by the German airmen with no regard for life. The youngest person killed was a 1-year-old baby and the oldest was an 82-year-old woman. Altogether, twenty people were killed.

On 26 January Aveton Gifford was bombed in a raid by five Focke-Wulf 190 aircraft. A 5-year-old girl, who had been evacuated from Plymouth, was killed outright. Twenty people were injured and nearly every home in the village sustained some kind of damage.

Rescue work carried on into the evening and the Home Guard patrolled St Andrew's Church to guard valuables from looters. The WVS provided 700 meals to villagers and helpers over the next couple of days.

Towards the end of January, the *Western Morning News* reported on the fish shortage in Plymouth. A fish hawker said, 'They want anything they can get but we can't get enough of anything with which to supply them.'

Queueing for foodstuffs, whether rationed or unrationed, had become a daily routine for every housewife and, as far as fish was concerned, the housewife appreciated its value in helping to eke out the meat ration and consequently joined the queues which began to form by the barrows and outside the shops long before the dealers came along with their wares. A woman hawker, who had a pitch near the Plymouth Pannier Market, told a *Western Morning News* reporter that she always found a queue of people awaiting her arrival. 'They are glad to get anything,' she confided, 'but generally ask first for hake, failing that whiting and then red mullet.'

On Saturday 30 January representatives of the United States Army presented Exeter with their flag and a commemorative plaque. The presentation took place at the Guildhall in Exeter. Detachments of the British and United States Army were cheered by thousands of onlookers who lined the route to the scene of the presentation. Heading the parade was an American military band, behind which was a detachment of American troops followed by a party of four soldiers carrying the Stars and Stripes.

Women salvage workers in Plymouth. Here, furniture has been salvaged from a house to be saved and stored away for safe keeping. Unfortunately, a lot of the saved items were later destroyed in further bombing attacks.

The Queen's Messengers Convoy ready with hot food. These were a familiar sight and were set up to feed the homeless and supply warm food and drink to people without electric and water supplies. The Queen's Messenger Food Convoys were named after Queen Elizabeth (the mother of today's Queen Elizabeth) who donated money for the first eighteen convoys.

The Queen's Messengers at Central Park, Plymouth. Here, a group of firemen enjoy a well-deserved mug of tea delivered by the Queen's Messengers Convoy. The side of their van reads, 'Food Flying Squad USA to Britain'. The Flying Squad was supplied by the American Committee for Air Raid Relief to Great Britain.

Queueing for rationed food. Huge queues would form for any kind of food that became available. Even a vague rumour could get a queue forming. Fruit wasn't rationed but was in very short supply. Exotic fruits such as bananas were rarely seen.

The Queen's Messengers at Home Park, Plymouth, handing out loaves. The Messengers were a lifeline to the many people who found themselves without homes, food or possessions. Originally called the 'Food Convoys,' they consisted of a few vehicles supplied with bread, basic food stuffs, water and a field kitchen.

The Queen's Messenger's van draws a crowd at St Budeaux in Plymouth. Many people became refugees in their own city. They had no homes to go to during the day and would spend their time in rest centres. Many would travel out into the countryside at night time to get away from the bombing and sleep in lorries, lanes or farms. In the city, the Queen's Messengers would make sure that they were well fed and had hot meals.

The band of the Devonshire Regiment and a detachment from the Royal Wiltshire Regiment completed the parade.

When the ceremony was over, the mayoress called for cheers for 'Our American friends' which was met by much enthusiasm from the crowds.

At the beginning of February the Kentisbeare Home Guard held a dance for the Royal Devon and Exeter Hospital and raised £9 9s. Meanwhile, contributions to the Exeter Diocesan and Central War Relief Fund exceeded £7,200 with a gift of £63 from St Peter's church, Tiverton.

Hit and run raids on Devon towns
On 13 February enemy planes were spotted heading towards Dartmouth. Bombs were dropped at Old Mill Creek near to the Royal Naval College. Another plane dropped a bomb close to the Butterwalk which wrecked buildings and left people trapped in the rubble. After ten hours, soldiers recovered the bodies of a mother and her children as well as those of four other people. All had been killed in the blast. At 4.30am, the body of a further woman was recovered.

Meanwhile, Torquay and Paignton had also come under attack. Phosphorous incendiary bombs were used by the Germans while attacking Torquay. On the same night, Plymouth was attacked again although this was its first night attack for eighteen months. A bomb dropped at Palmerston Street, Stoke left a huge crater and demolished two houses. Fifty others were badly damaged. Another bomb fell outside the Continental Hotel in Millbay. A dance had been going on at the time and, although the building was damaged, no-one was killed.

During an air-raid attack on Plymouth in February, six people were killed in the Stoke area of the city.

At 12.15pm on 26 February, eight FW190s planes machine gunned and bombed Exmouth killing the landlord of the Clarence Inn as well as the wife of the President of Exmouth Rugby Football Club. A bomb was dropped on Phillips Avenue to the north as well as at the Fulham Road junction of Exeter Road.

A 500kg bomb hit the town's shopping area. After demolishing several buildings, it exploded killing twenty people. Many had run for cover when they heard the Germans machine gunning the streets.

On 27 February German E-boats sank the minesweeper HMS *Harstad*, the anti-submarine vessel HMS *Lord Hailsham* and the cargo vessel *Moldavia*. Rescued survivors were taken to Dartmouth where they were met by lorries and other transport waiting to take them away. Later in the day, fourteen bodies were also landed at Dartmouth.

French sailors were billeted at Kingswear across from Dartmouth and were part of the 23rd MTB Flotilla of the Free French Naval Forces which consisted of eight motor torpedo boats moored by the Kingswear jetty. In the evening, the boats would head out into the English Channel searching for enemy vessels.

In the third week of February the Alphington Home Guard and Civil Defence Services organised a dance and whist drive which raised £39 2s for the Royal Devon and Exeter Hospital.

Fifty Royal Marines, who formed the King's Squad of Royal Marines, passed out at RM Barracks Stonehouse on 19 February 1943. They were inspected by the General Officer Commanding the Royal Marine Division. The squad were instructed by Sergeant R.J. Corry.

On Thursday 25 February Lady Baden-Powell visited the Girl Guides and Brownies at Exmouth. The next day she visited Exeter and the event was recorded in the *Western Morning News*. Addressing members and supporters of Exeter's Girl Guides in the Guildhall, Lady Baden-Powell, the Chief Guide, said in playing the game of Guides they were perhaps better than they knew, helping the girls to become the splendid women that were needed in our homes and national life.

She said that when the movement started, many people thought 'what a queer, cranky idea,' it was. 'Those people did not see that times were changing and women were coming forward to take their places beside the men.'

At the beginning of March, Devon launched an intensive campaign requesting volunteer labour to plant, lift and harvest potatoes. At a meeting of the County War Agricultural Executive Committee, a scheme was decided upon which organised labour from towns in the country on a part-time basis to meet the extreme shortage of workers. Volunteers were paid fixed wages.

On 3 March Mr Charles Williams MP who was speaking at the annual meeting of the St Mary Church and Babbacombe Conservative Club, said that, 'The more we bomb Germany, the more we reduce raids on this country. It is the best defence we have.'

Lady Baden-Powell arriving at Exmouth towards the end of February 1943. There, she visited contingents from Woodbury, Topsham, Budleigh Salterton, Littleham and Lympstone.

He went on to say that during the past three years, he had kept in close touch with the Under Secretary for Air and had played a part in securing the air defences that were already in place. He said that tip-and-run raids constituted a problem which affected every town on the coast and he thought British fighters should be as near to hand as possible to catch the enemy as they went out.

During March, American troops erected two Nissen Huts at Manadon Hill and at Victoria Road in Plymouth. They were to be used as social centres where dances and refreshments were offered. An 11-year-old girl sang at one of the dances and the Americans raised £100 for her to attend a singing school.

On Wednesday 10 March Robert White McFarlane, of 57 Alvington Street, Plymouth, and Sydney Crosscrete Camp, of 15 Woodville Road, Devonport, were charged with breaking and entering a store in Mill Street and stealing £1,025 10s 5d worth of women's clothing, the property of Messrs Spooners and Co Ltd.

The head storeman, Mr Charles W. Johns, said that he found the padlock with which he had secured the sliding doors had been removed and replaced with one of a similar design. He went into the stores and found that the contents of several boxes had been stolen.

Detective Constable Pearce stated that he had been sent to Hooper's Farm in Honicknowle and had recovered some of the articles from a bedroom. He later saw McFarlane and told him that he thought that he was responsible. McFarlane replied, 'I am sorry, I do not know anything about it.'

He was told that a quantity of the stolen clothing had been traced to a man called Basil Jones who told how it came into his possession. To this McFarlane replied, 'I may as well tell you the truth. I broke into Spooners with another man named Syd.'

Both men were committed for trial.

On 12 March, Salcombe came under attack trapping several people, including a sailor, under rubble.

During March, it was reported that a Devon and Cornwall Club had been formed at a prisoner of war camp in Germany which had fifty-six members. The president was Staff Sergeant Major C.W. Davis, RASC and the secretary was Lance Sergeant W.E. Richards, RA.

Lady Baden-Powell received an enthusiastic welcome at Plymouth on 3 March 1943. As Chief Guide, she was touring the West Country visiting Girl Guides and Brownies.

In a letter home, the secretary stated that the main objectives of the club were:

1. To enable men from the same town or district to meet and, if unknown to each other, to become acquainted.
2. To meet for the exchange and discussion of news from the two counties.
3. To promote social activities.
4. Mutual assistance.
5. To keep a record of prisoners from the two counties in order to facilitate the arranging of reunions on their return to the United Kingdom.

The Three Towns Club was also formed within the camp. Lance Sergeant Richards wrote: 'It would be appreciated if a summary of local news could be sent to us periodically, e.g. wartime activities of Argyle footballers, well-known boxers, wrestlers etc.'

American troops at the Palace Theatre in Union Street, Plymouth raised £27 towards the musical education of a 13-year-old girl from Devonport. The girl, Patricia Thomas, sang an impromptu song during the interval of an ENSA concert.

During April, Mr Charles H. Pillar of Duke Street, Tavistock, raised over £27 for the Red Cross Prisoners of War Fund. Meanwhile, the sum of £14 was raised by the Exmouth Stamp Club for the Red Cross Fund by a sale of stamps by auction and a donation of £4 7s 6d from the club's fund.

Jeeps and lorries outside The Salvation Army Sailors Home where US Navy operations were situated on the 3rd floor. The American Jeep was a popular site around Plymouth, a handy vehicle with a four-wheel drive. They were left-hand drive but the Americans soon got use to driving on our roads.

In connection with the Auxiliary Messenger Service, an Exeter City Police Flight of the Air Training Corps was formed.

American forces lend a hand

In the spring of 1943 Plymouth had its first experience of the American Army. They had been stationed in Britain for some time before their presence was felt in the South West. A whole division, the 29th, moved from Salisbury Plain to Devon and Cornwall and set up in barracks which had previously been used by British units. They were well equipped, well dressed and well mannered. They were kept under strict discipline and any misdemeanour was dealt with by their own officers or special courts.

The Americans were always ready to lend a hand. A classic example was the construction of 250-bed Naval Hospital at Manadon. In just two months, they had built the foundations, the camp and also equipped the hospital with everything it would need. Every section from the nuts and bolts to the stores and equipment came from the US. The foundations had proved a problem at first but these were made from the tons of rubble from the destroyed buildings in Plymouth.

The American Red Cross took over five of the large houses in Elliot Terrace in Plymouth, the terrace where Lord and Lady Astor lived, and turned them into a hostel for the troops. Plymouth became an important centre prior to the invasion of Europe and was visited by General Dwight Eisenhower on several occasions. His cavalcade

American troops shift rubble and debris in the centre of Plymouth. In the background is the city's Co-operative building.

US soldiers practising using a stirrup pump. There were so many American troops in Plymouth during and after 1943, that their presence swamped the few British soldiers still in the area. Both soldiers and sailors crowded the streets and shops. They had a respect for Plymouth and its people and for all that they had endured before the Americans' arrival.

of a large military car and armed motor-cycle riders was a sight to see and became quite well known in the city.

A newspaper article carried a story under the headline, WHAT AMERICANS BUY IN PLYMOUTH. It read:

Americans visiting Plymouth have experienced difficulty in buying souvenirs to take home but shop assistants find them cheerful customers and on the whole easy to please.

Among the first things they make for are view cards, now becoming very scarce. Many have shown their interest in trying to see as much as possible of this part of the world by searching for maps of Plymouth and Devonshire, both of which are difficult to obtain. Maps of Plymouth can only be bought on the production of a police permit.

Clothing and sweet rationing, of course, limits their range and the shops have only a small variety of fancy goods to offer. For their wives and sweethearts at home (or maybe their English girlfriend) they have picked mainly on cosmetics, handbags and flowers. In the bookshops, their choices have been confined chiefly to travel and literature on the West Country, plus a few novels.

Notepaper for writing home is an essential and from the stationers, they have also bought box-files, drawing instruments and rubber stamps. The china and glassware they have purchased is apparently for use in the messes. None of the hand painted china and pottery Americans were so fond of before the war is being made now.

Two American visitors who entered a fruiterer's shop on Mutley Plain saw some peaches for sale and told the shopkeeper they were the first they had seen since leaving their own country. They would like to have bought one but decided that 3s 6d was 'a bit dear'.

On Tuesday 4 May, the *Western Morning News* carried a report about the anniversary of Exeter's blitz. It stated that though far from complete, recovery had been sure. There had been healthy symptoms. Trade, which was the city's life-blood, had been returning in increasing volume. Many traders continued to suffer; others, including some who were blitzed, were re-established far more firmly than they had thought possible.

Such recovery could not have materialised without a communal effort. Traders gave the lead. Unhelped and even hampered by government departments in some instances, they bestirred themselves while the city still burned. With determination and enterprise, they set about the task of rehabilitation.

During May, John Reginald Barker, a radiographer of 3 Longbrook Street, Plympton St Maurice, applied to the South Western Conscientious Objectors' Tribunal at Bristol for exemption from military service stating that he objected to service on religious grounds. He believed that war was a direct denial of the true spiritual purpose of Jesus Christ. He was retained on the register on the condition that he continued in the occupation of a radiographer.

Meanwhile, Horace Edgar Francis, a maintenance hand and a member of the Brethren, of 6 Marlborough Road, Ilfracombe, also objected to combatant service on religious grounds. He was retained on the register and marked for non-combatant duties.

On 17 May, Teignmouth came under attack once more but escaped with little damage.

'Nazi raiders' claim more lives

The *Western Morning News* of Monday 17 May reported that fighters had chased 'Nazi raiders'. The article stated that thousands of people on the streets of Plymouth and the surrounding towns and villages had watched a thrilling pursuit of two enemy raiders by British fighters early on the previous Saturday afternoon. They did not know the result of that chase until some time later because raiders and defenders were eventually lost in the haze of distance as the machines raced away over the channel.

The first intimation of a 'kill' by our fighters was of when hundreds of people, listening to the opening of the Plympton 'Wings for Victory' Week, heard Air Vice Marshal G.R. Bromet say in a tribute to Fighter Command: 'Just before lunch today, Fighter Command gave you an example of driving away the enemy. Many of you saw part of that pursuit, which I am able to tell you resulted in an enemy aircraft being shot down.'

Later in the news bulletins, it was announced that one enemy raider was shot down after a 50-mile chase out over the sea and the second dived for safety.

When the machines were over Plymouth, they were too high to distinguish with the naked eye but their course could be followed by the vapour trails which each left in its wake. There were also bursts of gunfire from the ground defences to help in turning the raiders away. The two raiders had circled the city at tremendous height and were heading out to sea again when the vapour trails of the British fighters were seen coming up from the east. They were climbing at terrific speed and once having gained height were streaking after their quarry. It could be seen that they were rapidly overhauling the raiders when the haze obscured their trails.

On Sunday 30 May, a warm sunny day found many people strolling along the promenade at Torquay. Twenty-one FW190s appeared on the skyline flying at low level. They machine-gunned and bombed the town. Many were killed but Germans also lost their lives with five of their planes destroyed. One crashed into a terrace at Teignmouth Road. Forty-five people were killed by the Luftwaffe in the raid including twenty-one children at Sunday School as well as three of their teachers.

Thirteen people were killed in Plymouth on the night of 13 to 14 of June and 3,000 houses were destroyed or seriously damaged. A large number of unexploded bombs were dropped from a plane at low altitude. A 1,000 kg bomb crashed into the police headquarters at Greenbank bringing down 140 tons of masonry. The bomb lay unexploded on the landing outside the courtroom. Four enemy planes were brought down in the attack. One crashed at Stoke killing all the crew while another plane crashed soon after the crew had safely bailed out. They were soon caught.

On 14 June 1943 an enemy plane, a Junkers 88, crashed into the garden of a house at Stoke, Plymouth. The house was used as a hostel for the WRNS. This was the first time that an enemy plane had actually crashed within the city. The crew were killed and were later buried at Weston Mill cemetery with full honours. On the same night eighty high explosives were dropped on the city, although nearly half failed to explode. Thirteen people were killed in the raid and a considerable number were injured. At Plympton five people were killed and 600 houses damaged.

During the second half of 1943 and the first half of 1944, thousands of American troops occupied Devon and Cornwall complete with vehicles and equipment. There was much excitement when an American softball team played against a Canadian firefighters' team in Plymouth.

The *Western Morning News* of Saturday 19 June carried a story about a member of the Home Guard who had shot his father. It mentioned that a stern warning was given by Mr Justice Asquith at Exeter City Assize to Reginald Albert Ewings, aged 17, of the Exeter Home Guard, who pleaded guilty to a charge of maliciously wounding his father, Leonard Kimberley Ewings, at their home at 4 Ludwell Lane.

'I do not want you to think for a moment that you have not done a rash and foolish thing,' said his Lordship. 'You might by accident have been here on a much more serious charge.'

Mr G. Willett, prosecuting, said that following an argument the previous night between the father and mother, the accused had shot his father, a soldier home on leave, with his Home Guard rifle. He ran outside where he met a friend who was about to call on him and said: 'I have shot my father. I wish I had shot myself.' They went to the nearest policeman and Ewings said, 'I meant to kill him last night.'

Mr Willett said that Ewings had borne an excellent character and had been of great assistance to his mother under difficult circumstances. The occurrence had, perhaps, done the father some good. In a letter to his wife, from hospital, he wrote: 'Shake Reg by the hand, dear, and tell him not to worry. He has done me a good turn.'

Detective Inspector R.P. Rowland said Ewings was a good worker and his Home Guard commanding officer spoke highly of him.

Defending, Mr H.M. Pratt said that the root of the trouble was the drinking habits of the father. Accused was the eldest of the family at home and it fell to him to do whatever he could to protect his mother, brothers and sisters from the fury of his father. It was not strange that the crash had to come in some way. The circumstances were undoubtedly very extenuating.

Ewings was bound over for two years.

During June American army lorry drivers were taught the British highway code. Many of the US trucks were too wide for the country roads.

On Friday 2 July there was a public appeal for help regarding the harvest in Devon. Mr Hayter-Haymes, on submitting a report to the War Agricultural Committee stated: 'We have promise of a really remarkable harvest.'

Elsie Norton, a member of the Women's Land Army, thatching a rick of straw which had been threshed on a South Devon farm during June 1943.

He went on to say that soldier labour, which had been available the previous year, probably would not be available this time around and he appealed for the general public to assist farmers with the harvest.

On Monday 12 July Mr and Mrs W. Yeo, of Ebberly Dairy, Newport, Barnstaple, received a postcard from their son, Operator Wireless and Line Signalman W.H.J. (Billy) Yeo stating that he was a prisoner of war in Japanese hands and was quite well. Before joining the Royal Corps Signals as radio mechanic, Mr Yeo assisted his father at the Ebberly Dairy.

In July a large number of American officers attended a function given at the Abbey Hall by the Lord Mayor and Lady Mayor of Plymouth. American army nurses, Wrens, WAAF and members of the ATS joined in the dance in the lecture hall.

With buildings destroyed, major shops and businesses set up in the Pannier Market in Plymouth. The market was equipped with new stalls which were rentable at 3d per foot per day. Housed in the market were household names such as Woolworths, Marks and Spencers, Costers and Boots. On a busy day, over 30,000 people would flock to the market.

Tin Pan Alley in Plymouth. This was a temporary shopping area adjacent to the market. After their premises were destroyed in the blitz of 1941, major businesses like Marks and Spencers and Woolworths were given prime positions within the Pannier Market while smaller businesses operated from corrugated iron stalls situated in Drake Street.

Winners of the baby show at an Exminster fete during July 1943.

A trader operating from a handcart. With many buildings destroyed, businesses carried on as best as they could either setting up in smaller premises, which sometimes included someone's front room, or in makeshift Nissan huts.

The Western Times of Friday 23 July carried a report about supplementary labour in Devon for the harvest. It reported that a number of prisoners from Exeter Prison were to help with the corn harvest. So far as supplementary help was concerned, the Devon War Agricultural Committee was in a better position to assist the farmer than a year ago; 300 land girls were available from various centres to hire out to farms daily and it was hoped by the end of the month that this number would be increased to 500. The majority of girls had acquired practical experience of farm work.

Twelve schoolboy camps were being arranged and valuable assistance was to be given by part-time workers under the emergency land workers scheme. Prisoners of war from camps would also help and the War Agricultural Committee was prepared to hire out Irish workers who were in their employ. Soldier labour would depend upon the military situation. In East Devon, the local War Agricultural Committee were co-operating with the local traders in recruiting a number of auxiliary workers, all of whom had been absorbed in some kind of spare-time farming work. This was typical of what was happening at various centres throughout the county.

There was a fear that the Germans might attack Burrator Reservoir on Dartmoor in retaliation for the earlier Dambusters attacks. Anti-mine nets were placed 20ft upstream, close to the face of the dam.

On 12 August, a German raid on Plymouth killed forty-one while another ninety were seriously injured. Bombs fell between Laira to Devonport, luckily again, many failed to explode. Several bombs fell in Central Park, near to the anti-aircraft gun site in the corporation cabbage patch. All failed to explode. American troops stationed at Crownhill helped the Civil Defence forces rescuing casualties and doing what they could.

The *Western Morning News* of Wednesday 18 August carried a story under the headline DEVONS IN SICILY. It noted that the participation of men of the Devonshire Regiment in the fighting in Sicily had already been announced and letters had reached Great Britain from some of the Devon men on the island. An officer wrote that the Devons had done very well and that the corps commander had congratulated the battalion on its work. The men were reported to be all very fit and cheerful especially now that they had driven the Germans out of their strong position.

During the summer, the Americans established naval bases at both Instow and Appledore. The USS *President Warfield* accommodated US naval personnel and was moored up in the River Torridge.

Most of the accommodation at Ilfracombe was given over to American servicemen before they moved to purpose-built camps at Braunton and Saunton. More and more troops arrived in the area in preparation of Operation Overlord (the planned D-Day landings). US army vehicles filled the streets of Ilfracombe and belonged to the units of the 156th Infantry Division.

In August, Plymouth was bombed again. This time, forty-one men, women and children were killed as well as another ninety injured.

Many civilian evacuees arrived in Salcombe and had to be housed. At the same time, an American Naval Construction Battalion arrived in the town and set up an amphibious base. The Americans eventually outnumbered the locals, many of who were away fighting in the war.

A crashed enemy aircraft in a field close to houses on the outskirts of Plymouth.

The Americans set up a school for amphibious training and gun support at HMS *Britannia* at Dartmouth and built workshops on Coronation Park. Altogether, 3,684 Americans were housed in the college as well as in huts and tents within the college grounds.

A small naval store was set up at Tiverton and a Weapon Training School was established at Woolacombe. Meanwhile, the Combined Operations Experimental Establishment took up residence in Appledore.

Projects like the Great Panjandrum were trialled on Instow beach. The weapon consisted of two giant wheels which could travel at up to 60 miles an hour and explode when it struck a concrete defence.

During August, members of the US Army collected £9 8s for the Prince of Wales hospital.

In September Mrs Cane of Grafton Road, Newton Abbot, raised £9 6s for the Red Cross by selling two lemons which had been sent to her by her son who was stationed in Sicily.

On Thursday 9 September Barnstaple magistrates imposed a fine of 24s on Mary Homer, a married woman, for breaching black-out regulations at 6 Pengelly's Court, Barnstaple.

On the same day, Jack Boyce Diamond, aged 21, a soldier, was charged at Torquay with stealing nine chickens to the value of £4 10s. He was fined £2 and ordered to make restitution to the owner.

The American Red Cross supplying warm food and tea. The American Red Cross took over five of the large houses in Elliot Terrace, the terrace where Lord and Lady Astor lived, and turned them into a hostel for the troops. Plymouth became an important centre prior to the invasion of Europe and was visited by General Dwight Eisenhower on several occasions. His cavalcade of a large military car and armed motor-cycle riders was a sight to see and became quite well known in the city.

John Luscombe, aged 14, helping his father on his farm at Higher Holditch, Kingsbridge. He left school to take up the work. His brother, Michael, aged 7, can also be seen riding his pony, Peggy.

The *Western Morning News* of Friday 10 September carried a story of two girls' efforts to aid the Prisoners' Fund. It stated that two children, Dorothy Jean Penhaligon, of 29 Union Street, St Thomas, Exeter, and Mary Elizabeth Stapley, of 61 Cecil

Road, Exeter, had raised £6 for the Red Cross and St John Prisoners of War Fund by exhibiting a golliwog made by a trained nurse while she was undergoing treatment in hospital. One of the girls was the nurse's niece. A doll and a lemon were prizes in a competition arranged by Miss Darch and realised £5 13s and £1 respectively for the fund. They were given by Mrs K. Knight and Mrs Toy. A darts competition, organised by St Anne's Well Brewery Co Ltd, Exeter, raised £7 8s for the fund.

On Sunday 12 September William Henry Phillips of Clyst Road, Broadclyst died at the Royal Devon and Exeter Hospital after being hit by an army lorry near his home.

Dawlish Flag Day, on behalf of the Soldiers', Sailors' and Airmen's Families' Association, organised by E.A. Lamacraft, raised £46. A Gift Day on behalf of Dawlish Parochial Church Funds, realised £76 6s.

In September, to commemorate the Italian surrender, a gentleman from Littleham near Exmouth presented each of the schoolchildren living in the village with saving stamps worth 2s 6d.

During Plymouth and District Deaf and Dumb Mission and Institute Flag Day, £84 4s was collected.

Sergeant Gay of the Plymouth Civil Defence Service trained American soldiers in the ways of British firefighting during September.

At the beginning of October, it was reported that Lord Astor had been invited to assume the responsibility of the duties of Lord Mayor of Plymouth for the fifth year in succession, a record for the city. His lordship accepted the invitation. Viscountess Astor, MP, continued her work as the Lady Mayoress.

The decision to invite Lord Astor to continue office was unanimous. Each member of the committee, in turn, bore tribute to the services that the Lord Mayor had rendered

An American pilot, with his Jeep, who had been posted to Bolt Head during September 1943 as air support for D-Day.

A search is made for any sign of life amongst the rubble of a destroyed building in Plymouth. Civil Defence workers were a liaison between the Navy, Army, Air Force and the civilian population. The town Clerk, Colin Campbell, was the controller of the ARP.

Miss Maureen Rogers erects the indicator of the Turnchapel train, of which she is conductress, before it leaves Plymouth in October 1943.

the city. Alderman Dunstan expressed the hope that the fifth term of office would be marked by the proclamation of a victorious peace. Thanks were tendered to Lord Astor for his service to the city. Accepting. Lord Astor said he recognized the honour that had been conferred upon him. He hoped to help in laying the foundations for the replanning of the city. He trusted that the bells of peace would ring in his coming year of office.

Mutiny at a US camp and a problem with fleas

The *Yorkshire Evening Post* of Friday 15 October reported on a court-martial at Paignton. The article told that fourteen soldiers were charged at an American court-martial at Paignton, Devon with mutiny at a United States camp in Cornwall. They were also charged with shooting with intent to murder two American army police sergeants and other people in the square of a town; with rioting and unlawfully taking and firing firearms and making inflammatory statements in the presence of other soldiers.

Each of the men pleaded not guilty to a total of ten charges or specifications.

The prosecuting officer said that on Sunday night, a group of soldiers, including the accused, had been frequenting public houses and agreed between them to stand against other soldiers.

An interesting story about a fire guard and fleas appeared in the *Western Morning News* of Tuesday 26 October. It noted that a fire guard who absented himself from his duty in order to bring to the notice of the authorities the 'enormous number of fleas' at his post, appeared at Exeter Police Court. Percival Jarratt, of 127 Wardrew Road, Exeter, admitted being absent from his post, at a former Baptist Chapel in Exeter.

Inspector K. Steer said PC Underhill visited the chapel and found Jarratt had not reported. When interviewed, the defendant said, 'I have my own reasons for not being there.' Asked to explain, he said, 'Not now.'

Jarratt told the bench, 'When I was ordered to go there I found the place extremely dirty. There were three beds, one of which it was impossible to use. A constable told me that one of the party had to stay awake all night, so that only two beds would be needed.'

The blankets were full of fleas and he had written in the log-book many times about it, as well as complaining to three police constables who called and to the senior fire guard.

'I didn't turn up,' added Jarratt, 'because I knew I should be prosecuted and the matter brought up. The conditions were atrocious.'

Inspector Steer told the bench that the basket-making business carried on seemed to entice fleas.

The senior fire guard for the group agreed that the fleas were 'no doubt there'. The floor was washed through with disinfectant and the blankets were cleaned once a month. On an average, twenty-eight or thirty people slept in them between cleaning.

Mr A.C. Reed MP (from the bench) stated, 'They can't be quite as they should be.'

The witness replied, 'No, I quite agree. You can't get rid of the fleas.'

The chairman said that the case would be dismissed and the bench would see that the complaint was brought to the notice of the proper authority.

A young hero

Towards the end of October tributes were paid to a boy at the close of a conference by the Otter Group of the British Legion at Exmouth. A silver watch and chain was presented to John Middleton, a 12-year-old Exmouth boy, in recognition of his courage and resource during an air raid.

Major A.E. Jones, the chairman of the Exmouth branch of the Legion, said John with his brother Cecil, age 10 years, were in bed unwell on the third floor of a house when machine-gun bullets started whistling into their room, followed by a bomb explosion close at hand. They immediately got behind the door just as the whole building gave way and they found themselves nearly buried in debris with Cecil trapped by the door.

John, recovering himself, came downstairs to the second floor, where he found Mrs Field trapped with head injuries. He did all he could to help her and then went to the ground floor and brought the rescue party to their aid.

On coming down to the ground floor a second time, he heard Mr P. Mathews and Mr P. Evans (both officers of the British Legion), who had been trapped and almost buried in the debris of the business premises, calling for help. He again found a party and led them to where they were. Making the presentation, Colonel G. Lestock Thornton, president of the Exmouth branch, told John Middleton that he could regard the gift as they in the Army would regard a Distinguished Conduct Medal won on the battlefield. Messrs Mathews and Evans (who were mainly responsible for the gift) were the first to thank the recipient and shake him by the hand.

In November, the United States Naval Amphibious Base was set up in Plymouth. Its main purpose was for the training and reception of troops taking part in various exercises in the region in the run up to D-Day.

Plymouth was bombed on the morning of 16 November, when eighteen people were killed and sixty were injured. Forty houses were destroyed and extensive damage was caused to over 2,000 homes. The bombs fell on Devonport, Pennycross, Mannamead and Stoke.

The Western Times of Friday 26 November reported a story about two North Devon men who were in court for unlawfully receiving food. It mentioned that John Henry

An exceptional haul of fish at Plymouth during November 1943. Many housewives rushed to buy what they could.

American soldiers help with salvage work in Plymouth. A small boy watches from the right. Children were fascinated by the Americans, their only previous contact with them would have been from watching extravagant Hollywood movies at the many local cinemas.

Rippon, a lorry driver, of Brook Cottage, Landkey, and John Davie, a farm labourer, of the Village, Yarnscombe were brought in front of the Magisterial Bench in the County Police Court, Barnstaple, on the previous Wednesday. With them, were displayed tins of apricots, raisins, sultanas, currants, tea, rice, lard and peanut butter etc. The items were alleged to have been unlawfully received from Army camps by the pair. Both defendants pleaded guilty but stated that the articles were placed on their lorry by soldiers when they called at the camps for pigs' swill and that the soldiers told them to do what they liked with them and they paid nothing for the goods. 'The stuff was chucked at us,' they added.

Superintendent P. Melhuish said that the soldiers concerned had been dealt with by the authorities.

Rippon, against whom there was a previous conviction for stealing, was fined £5 and Davie £3.

The paper shortage meant that no Christmas decorations were available in shops but people made do with improvised decorations made with recycled items.

In December, the American troops threw Christmas parties for thousands of schoolchildren in Plymouth. They fetched the children from their schools in their Jeeps and lorries and took them back again after the party. The soldiers paid for the parties themselves and, as they weren't restricted by rationing, there were plenty of chocolates and sweets and every child came away clutching a toy or a doll.

The *Western Morning News* of Tuesday 28 December carried details of Devon's pantomimes. It mentioned that 'Cinderella', the ever-popular pantomime beloved by young and old, charmed large audiences in Plymouth, Exeter and Torquay.

Plymothians wishing to put some peacetime touches to their wartime festivities needed only go to the Palace Theatre where Miss Cora Craven as Cinderella put everything into the part. At the opening, every little girl in the audience wished she was Cinderella. Her Prince Charming was the lovely Miss Mari Kenealy.

Buttons, popular with the children, was played by Mr Harry Seltzer. In true pantomime fashion, he soon had his young audience, and the older ones too, laughing at his slapstick comedy and his singing of such songs as 'I wish I had a banana again'.

D-Day rehearsals at Slapton Sands during 1943.

The two Ugly Sisters, played by Mr John Powe and Miss Maud Cowderry, had particular ill-fortune. Having to suffer under the names of Arabella and Clorinda, their faces and tempers did not help them when they tried to capture the heart of the prince. A quick change of scene and the audience were able to watch Jim Dellas's dogs performing some amazing tricks. The clever animals did everything from pushing their friends in prams to selecting on cards the right solutions to arithmetical problems. The chorus included Babette's Twelve Plymouth Babes. The local girls took part in one of the most beautiful of the ten scenes, the Fairy Ballet.

On 29 December troops accidentally burnt down Clovelly Court. Also in December American troops knocked over a pony with one of their Jeeps. The pony, called Bambi, belonged to Mrs Margaret Clarke and its hind leg was broken. Four departments of the US Army helped put the pony's leg in a splint and, eventually, it recovered fully.

Towards the end of December a huge children's party was laid on by the American Red Cross. It was held at Elliott Terrace on the Hoe in Plymouth. Troops delivered boxes which they'd marked 'Save your candy for the children's party'. The children of the volunteer staff were invited as well as fifty poor children.

In late 1943, in preparation for D-Day, the British government set up a training ground at Slapton Sands. The beach was chosen for its gravelly similarity to the proposed landing point, Utah beach. Over 3,000 residents were evacuated from the area. Some had previously never left their villages. Landing exercises started to take place during December.

On 31 December, the 29th Infantry Division of the American forces trained as part of Operation Duck at Slapton. The exercise involved performing various amphibious manoeuvres.

CHAPTER 6

1944 – D-Day

In January 1944 the US Army set up a camp at Vicarage Road, Saltash Passage, Plymouth, in preparation for the D-Day landings. The whole operation was top secret and from May 1944, anyone who wanted to visit relatives in the area had to apply for a permit and was escorted to the address by military police. They also had to give a specific time when they would be leaving.

Children in the area loved the American troops and would pester them for sweets, chewing gum, chocolate, food and cocoa etc. The Americans weren't affected by rationing and were very generous to the locals, especially the children.

The large majority of troops in Plymouth were from the 29th Armoured Division which went on to land at Omaha and Utah beaches, the codenames for the main landing points for American troops on 6 June 1944.

The first half of 1944 saw American troops training at Slapton.

The *Gloucestershire Echo* of Saturday 8 January reported a chance reunion of two brothers who might have met on different sides in battle. They had met at Cullompton, Devon, one was a US soldier and the other was an Italian prisoner of war. There was an

Troops stationed near Saltash Passage. The Royal Albert Bridge can be seen in the background. In January 1944 the US army set up a camp at Vicarage Road in preparation for the D-Day landings.

extraordinary reunion, with many touches of Italian emotionalism. The brother on the winning side, had left Italy many years previously and had become an American citizen.

During January, the Mayor of Exeter received £1 16s for the City Air Raid Relief Fund from the Women's Auxiliary of Cornwall, Devon and Somerset Association of Vancouver.

Recruitment for the Land Army was reopened during January. Women between the ages of 17 and 35 were required for milking and other responsible jobs. Applicants were asked to obtain the permission of their employment exchange before applying to the Land Army County Office. Farmers requiring help had to make an application to the same office and make their needs known.

In the third week of January, Mr A. Hillson complained that farmers and their workers were getting wet feet because of the shortage of rubber boots. He raised the point at a meeting of the Exeter branch of the National Farmers' Union and stated that there were at least 2,000 people waiting for them. He suggested that the executive committee take the matter up with the War Agricultural Executive Committee and, if necessary, with the Board of Trade.

Mr A. Porter, the county secretary, said that protests had been made against the issue of ankle boots which were useless for farming work. Mr Colin D. Ross, chief executive officer of the WAEC, sympathised with Mr Hillson and assured him that every effort was being made to get the rubber boots. It was decided to ask the executive committee to request headquarters to press for a supply as soon as possible.

During January a pantomime called 'The Old Lady who lived in a Shoe' was performed for American servicemen at the Octagon Youth Club in Stonehouse, Plymouth.

At the beginning of February, collections were made for the Red Cross in Exeter's three cinemas. Over £1,213 was raised for the fund. Meanwhile, the Young Farmers of Winkleigh raised £24 13s for the Royal Devon and Exeter Hospital by holding a dance.

It was reported on 4 February that a black retriever dog had raised over £2,000 for the Southern Railway Orphanage at Woking. The dog had been a familiar sight at the Central Station in Exeter for eight years and always carried a collection box on his back. He had previously been awarded five silver medals and one gold medal and during February was awarded fourteen more medals at a special presentation by Lord Mamhead. The dog was nine-and-a-half years old and to date had raised £2,311 assisted by Guard John Bovett.

Land girls taking care of fruit trees at an orchard at Whimple during January 1944.

The Field Hospital at Manadon, Plymouth, which opened on 12 February 1944. It was built to provide medical facilities for American servicemen. It stood on rubble brought by the servicemen from the blitzed city and took two months to construct.

Life under the Gestapo

A story was featured in the *Western Morning News* of Monday 14 February:

Experiences of 21 months as a civilian internee in Germany were described by Mrs Mary Merritt in a lecture at the Art Gallery, Plymouth, on Saturday.

For six years, Mrs Merritt was in business in Antwerp. 'It was a shock to find one lovely morning that German planes were over the city and German bombs were dropping,' she said.

They quitted Antwerp and got to Ostende, where there was indescribable chaos owing to refugees. There was no hope of getting to England, so they went on and made for the French frontier, which was closed when they arrived.

'When people fainted, they could not fall down as there was no room. They were just propped up by the crowd,' she said. Most of the refugees were poorly clothed and shod, and many had no food. They had no idea where they were going, they just wandered along.

The Germans overtook them, said Mrs Merritt, and they returned to Antwerp, where they were put under strict supervision.

That winter they were allowed a quarter of a pound of bread a day. They never had any potatoes and the butchers' shops opened about once a fortnight. There was no butter but they had about 100 grams of oatmeal and the same amount of some kind of rice product. Vegetables were at exorbitant prices. Unrationed goods were unobtainable.

In April 1941 she was taken to Gestapo headquarters, where there were other prisoners. They were lined up and taken to Aachen, where they were given some food and later taken to a railway station, where they were made to stand back to back with soldiers round them. They travelled through the night and were transferred to a bus, which eventually swung through large gates of a lunatic asylum, partly filled with lunatics and partly filled with British subjects.

Mrs Merritt said they had good quarters and became quite used to the life, which was dull. The camp commandant used to arrange entertainments for them and they were also allowed to go for walks in escorted 'crocodiles'.

In August 1942 an official arrived and told them that owing to the atrocious treatment of prisoners in the British Empire, he was forced to take reprisals. About 80 of them were consequently moved into the crypt. There was so many beds in the crypt that it was difficult to move.

Large numbers of Polish Jews came to the camp in a distressing condition. In many cases, they had been transit prisoners for six weeks. A transit prisoner, explained Mrs Merritt, was hurled into a train in the morning, travelled all day, and was taken to a prison at night. They were not allowed to take off their clothes and were glad to get to the prison and settle down.

Another batch of prisoners from ghettoes in Poland, including many children under seven who were greyish green in colour, arrived on New Year's Day in 1942. The children were so frightened that they would not talk to anyone for some time. By that time food was very poor but Red Cross parcels turned up nearly every week. When we had had no letters from home for some time, it was very cheering to see the familiar labels on the tins,' she said.

Mrs Merritt said that only thirty-one prisoners returned to England from her camp. They travelled in ox wagons. It took them five days and five nights to get to Portugal. When she eventually reached a Scottish port, she could not believe her eyes at the sight of so many goods in the shop windows.

'You do not know how much you have to be thankful for,' she concluded. 'When people go overseas after the war, they will be shocked that people could live under such conditions and still remain sane.'

During February, the Barnstaple Rural Council refused a request from the military authorities to open cinemas on Sunday for the troops. Mr J.E. Pile, in support of the request, said that he preferred the cinema to the public house. Mr Hocking, opposing, said that there were plenty of places of worship open for the troops to attend. Mr R. Thomas said that it was disgraceful that there was any opposition to the proposal and said that the council were happy for the men to fire guns but not relax at the cinema. The chairman stated that what the men appreciated more than anything was an invitation into people's homes.

An inquest at the beginning of March into the death of a soldier from Tavistock found that no-one was to blame. Private Geoffrey Percy John Adams, aged 25, a single man, of 3 Railway Cottages, Trelawney Road, Tavistock, was fatally injured when dispatch riding near Salisbury on the previous Monday. He died at the hospital the next day from multiple injuries. Evidence given showed that deceased was motor cycling near Salisbury, when he collided with a motor milk lorry, owned by Nestles Products Ltd.

Left: *One of the small tugs, belonging to the US Army, which was moored at Richmond Wharf and was used to move larger vessels in and out of port.*

Right: *Squadron Leader F.R. Derry leaving Buckingham Palace, during March 1944, after receiving the DFC. He lived at Newton Ferrers and is pictured with his daughter.*

The *Western Morning News* of Saturday 25 March carried a story about a farmer who failed to enrol in the Home Guard. A fine of £2, with costs of 5s, was imposed by Ashburton magistrates on Jonathan Cock, aged 47, of Younghouse Farm, Ashburton, for failing to comply with a direction to enrol in the Home Guard.

Through Mr H.A.T. Coles, of Torquay, the defendant pleaded guilty and said that there had been a misunderstanding, by which he had appealed against the enrolment to the Devon War Agricultural Committee instead of the Appeals Tribunal.

Mr C. Field Fisher, also of Torquay, for the Ministry of Labour, said that the War Agricultural Committee had investigated the defendant's appeal and decided against it. He had refused to sign an enrolment form on the grounds that he was engaged in agricultural work, that labour was short, and that he was already fully occupied with other Civil Defence duties.

Mr Cole said that the defendant had a farm of sixty acres and he took over other grazing land and had forty head of cattle. He was virtually single-handed on the farm.

In answer to the bench, the defendant said his Civil Defence duties consisted of being in charge of a rest centre at Broadhempston and he was chairman of the committee.

Announcing the decision of the bench, the chairman considered that the National Service officer might have drawn the defendant's attention to the fact that he should have applied for notice of appeal against enrolment.

In the week commencing 27 March, £120 was raised at Bishopsteignton for the Aid-to-China Fund. A flag day raised £10 3s 6d and the Women's Institute bring-and-buy, with toys made by Courtlands School in Lindridge, raised £55 1s 4d. Whist drives and dances raised £20 10s.

Towards the end of March, performances of 'Twelfth Night' by pupils of Totnes County School for Girls raised £76 5s 1d for the Merchant Navy Comforts Fund.

Slapton Sands tragedy

Exercise Tiger took place at Slapton during April and May as preparation for the D-Day landings. On the morning of 28 April a practice assault resulted in the deaths of 639 American soldiers and sailors when enemy E-boats armed with torpedoes, alerted by heavy radio traffic in Lyme Bay, attacked three Landing Ship Tanks (LSTs), flat-bottomed assault ships capable of carrying several hundred men, lorries and tanks. Two were sunk and a third managed to limp back to Dartmouth. An error in radio frequencies and the absence for repair of a British Navy destroyer added to the tragedy. Deaths also occurred because of incorrectly worn lifejackets by Army personnel.

Because of the impending invasion of Northern Europe, the losses were shrouded in secrecy and those who survived were forbidden to speak about the incident on pain

Some of the survivors from the Slapton Sands exercise in April 1944 at the Vicarage Road Camp at Plymouth. They were Alexander Brown, Tom Clark, Fred Beattie, Ed Panter, James Murdock, Gene Eckstam, Bernard Carey, Doug Harlander and Scoffy Gill. They were later sent to Exeter for new uniforms and then sent to different detachments in readiness for D-Day.

Edinburgh Road Camp in Devonport was built in ten days on blitzed ground at Fore Street. It accommodated Rear Admiral D. Moon (US Army) and his staff who were drafted to Plymouth from Africa in the spring of 1944. Rear Admiral Moon commanded Group 2 of the 11th Amphibious Force.

of court martial. The tragedy was covered up for many years afterwards, although locals remembered seeing bodies at the time.

In the spring of 1944, Plymouth and other areas in Devon had one of the severest shortages of beer during the war. Devon Cider proved a popular replacement and went down well with American troops in the area who called it 'Invasion Juice'.

The *North Devon Journal* of Thursday 20 April reported on the Salute a Soldier campaign. It mentioned that Brigadier R.J.P. Wyatt had officially opened Ilfracombe and District's 'Salute the Soldier' Week on the previous Saturday. He took the salute on the Capstone Front in a parade of British and US forces, Home Guard, Civil Defence Services and Youth organisations. Thousands of residents and a large number of visitors watched the procession as it marched through the flag-and-bunting-bedecked streets to the music of several bands.

Ilfracombe and district's target was £150,000 to maintain and equip a base hospital for twelve months. Combe Martin hoped to contribute £15,000.

Mr F.G. Reed, the Chairman of the Area Savings Committee, when interviewed on the Saturday, said: 'We realise the need of doing all in our power to alleviate the suffering of those who may be wounded in the coming campaigns. Again, we have been asked to lead North Devon. Let us by our united endeavours show our appreciation in a practical manner of the efforts made on our behalf by the men and women of the Army.'

Professor Patrick Abercrombie and Lord Astor. Abercrombie had earlier visited Plymouth on 19 October 1941 at the invitation of Lord Astor and the members of the Emergency Committee. He was already heavily involved with the plans for reconstructing London but stayed the weekend with the Astors at their home in Elliot Terrace on the Hoe and commented that the view of the Hoe was the only part of Plymouth that he was familiar with. He visited again in 1944 as the plans were finalised.

The General Post Office, sub post offices, banks and official selling centres were busy on the Saturday morning. Many large purchases were reported. Children were among the earliest customers. The amount subscribed on the day was £25,000 and at closing time on the following Tuesday, £55,000 had been raised.

During April, the *Western Morning News* appealed for books for members of the US Navy stationed in Plymouth. Novels and detective stories were especially wanted.

Professor Abercrombie visited Plymouth to put forward his proposals for the rebuilding of the city. The Plan for Plymouth was published on 27 April 1944. Long before the war had ended, it was realised that Plymouth could not be rebuilt as it was before the war. The damage was too severe and long before the blitz, the roads were already suffering from severe traffic congestion. The proposal put forward was to clear the lot and start again with a modern, spacious city with wide roads.

On 30 April 1944, the bus depot in Plymouth received a direct hit. Three fire watchers sheltering there were killed and sixteen people were seriously injured. There was severe damage to the depot and several of the buses were totally destroyed.

American troops helping to clear away the rubble of a destroyed building in Plymouth during 1944.

Members of an American anti-aircraft gun crew positioned in the bombed centre of Plymouth during 1944. Charles Church can be seen in the background.

The bombed Western National Bus Depot at Prince Rock, Plymouth on 30 April 1944. There was severe damage to the depot and several of the buses were totally destroyed.

American crews supplying stores etc were housed in huts at Martin's Wharf in Plymouth. Here, one crew is seen displaying the American flag.

The last bombs fell on the city on 30 April 1944.

Plymouth and ports along the coastline had become home to a large encampment of American troops. Many parts were no-go areas for civilians. Waterways were filled with American ships and tents occupied any open spaces to accommodate the troops. Roads and lanes were lined with thousands of boxes of ammunition in preparation of the invasion of France. Although there was an information blackout, it became apparent to Plymothians that a major operation was about to take place.

Left: *Improvised Nissan huts. It would be many years before there were enough premises to house all of Plymouth's traders and Nissen huts sprung up all over the centre as a temporary measure. These were small, cramped and damp but served their purpose.*

Right: *Lance Corporal W. Ball of East Street, Okehampton, with his police dog, Blackie, in May 1944. Dogs were trained to be used to guard food and fuel at army camps in the Middle East, North Africa and Italy.*

The *Western Morning News* of Friday 12 May told of a Devon soldier guarding fuel and food. It stated that Lance Corporal William Ball, of 95 East Street, Okehampton, was a regular soldier with eight years' service to his credit.

I went to France in late 1939 with the Fourth Medium Regiment Royal Artillery. The move up into Belgium saw us stationed with our 6-inch howitzers near Brussels. Life had been very quiet for many months previously and moving over from a comparatively peaceful life to the conditions of chaos and confusion consequent upon the German invasion of the Low Countries was almost too swift a change to get used to in the time we had at our disposal.

Some day the whole story of the Expeditionary Force in France will be told. For the time being, I only know my own little part of it. The last position which our battery held was at a place called Ronque. We had about 75 rounds per gun left. All that we had, we flung at the Germans, leaving only a round or two to destroy the guns before we withdrew.

I felt at the time there was something very ominous in that self-destruction. It's a way back, not a way forward. But then, that's what Dunkirk was, and the climb upwards since has been long, if none the less sure.

For several months after the evacuation of Dunkirk, I was one of the crews manning coastal guns in the West of England. Those were the days of the Battle of Britain. Shortly after this, I had a bit of bad luck at Salisbury. I had a head-on collision with a motor ambulance. I was driving a motor cycle at the time. My left shoulder was broken and I was laid up for several weeks as a result.

I came overseas to North Africa in mid-1943 as a free reinforcement for artillery.

Towards the end of the year, I was sent to a military dog training centre. The success which had attended these establishments in guarding Army food and fuel dumps in the Middle East had prompted their use in North Africa and Italy. I think they will do pretty well in the work for which they are intended. Most of the animals which we have trained out here have been sent out from England. Largely, they have been lent to the Army from civilian owners and as a result their intelligence is high and they catch on to the work with amazing rapidity.

I hope to go out to Italy or elsewhere pretty soon now with a team.

On the lead up to the Allied invasion of Normandy, General Montgomery visited Plymouth on 26 May and spoke at a meeting of American officers at the Odeon cinema in Plymouth.

The *Western Morning News* of Thursday 1 June carried a story about housewives' assistance to soldiers. It noted that members of the Honicknowle WVS group of housewives organised a garden party at Warwick Park, Honicknowle, in aid of Plymouth's 'Salute the Soldier' Week.

It was opened by Chief Commander K. Acland, ATS, supported by Mrs Mckay Forbes, the head of the Houswives' Service of the WVS. A children's fancy dress parade was judged by Mrs Lorne Sayers, the Devon vice-president of the Red Cross Society, and Colonel R.S. Stafford, BBC. Mr Harry Grose was compère. Professor W.T. Lloyd provided a Punch and Judy show and performed some conjuring tricks

American troops gathered in Plymouth on 26 May 1944 for a briefing of the assault plans for Normandy; the talk was given by General Bernard Montgomery. The Odeon cinema can be seen in the background.

An American jazz band taking part in 'Salute the Soldier' week, marching by Plymouth Guildhall in 1944.

American troops prepare to leave for Normandy from Turnchapel in Plymouth.

and there were pony rides and a nursery for the children. A number of stalls offering strawberries, among other things, also proved an attraction.

In the evening, a play, written, produced and acted by the Honicknowle housewives was performed. The Deputy Lady Mayoress of Plymouth (Mrs W.J.W. Modley) and Mrs E. Wordley, head of Plymouth WVS, also attended.

The Salute the Soldier Week began in Plymouth on 3 June. It was opened by Baron Chatfield, the Admiral of the Fleet, and hoped to raise funds for members of the armed forces.

A unit of the 456th Battalion was stationed at Woodland Fort in Plymouth and part of the unit guarded the camp at Vicarage Road and the Royal Albert

The Americans had their Naval Base at Hamoaze House at Mount Batten but they also had an important Naval Advance Base in the Cattewater, Plymouth, where they occupied the whole frontage from Laira Bridge to Sutton Pool. After the Normandy landings, some of America's biggest warships came to Devonport Dockyard for repairs. These included the battleships Arkansas, Texas *and* Nevada.

Bridge. Many of them became friends with the locals. Saltash Passage residents all had ID cards but were issued with an extra yellow Certificate of Residence Card. It proved that the owner lived in the area and was issued because of the secrecy building up to the D-Day landings.

D-Day

Operation Overlord was the code name for the Battle of Normandy, the Allied invasion of France. Operation Neptune was the name given to the landings which took place at five key points in France codenamed Omaha, Utah, Gold, Juno and Sword. The American troops landed at Utah and Omaha and were made up of forces based all over the West Country.

As D-Day approached, some 36,000 American troops left Plymouth in two waves. The first were to land at Utah Beach and were made up of troops stationed at Brixham, Dartmouth, Salcombe and Plymouth. In total, 865 ships left from nine ports in Plymouth, under the command of Rear Admiral Don P. Moon on board USS *Bayfield*. A further 110 vessels left from Plymouth carrying American troops from the VII Corps of the 4th Infantry Division. They would be among the first troops to land at Utah Beach. More than 23,000 men belonging to the US 4th Infantry Division landed at Utah.

The assault on Omaha Beach was made by 1st and 29th Division troops and US Rangers. The first waves met fierce opposition and sustained more than 2,400

The smiling faces of American troops as they prepare to leave Saltash Passage in Plymouth on D-Day.

casualties. Strong winds and tides blew their landing craft off course, almost all the amphibious tanks were lost and the troops had to cross from the shoreline to the bluffs exposed to withering enfilade fire from German guns on the cliffs.

Together the British, Canadians and Americans landed about 156,000 troops in Normandy on 6 June either on the five landing beaches or by parachute and glider and established a beachhead from which they went on to liberate Europe.

US Commander C.D. Edgar headed the troops which included seven divisions made up of 25,000 men together with 4,429 landing vehicles.

On 6 June 1944 local residents in Saltash Passage, Plymouth awoke to find the area unusually quiet and found the American forces had departed leaving only a baseball bat which was kept as a souvenir by Graham Langston, the Unigate milkman in the area. The scene was the same all over Plymouth. Waterways which the previous day had been full of American troops and their ships were now empty as the Army headed towards the beaches of France to take part in the D-Day landings. More than 155,000 American,

American troops in Plymouth preparing for D-Day.

British and Canadian troops landed on the beaches of Normandy. The landings eventually resulted in a decisive Allied victory and ultimately led to the end of the war.

Plymouth became the main receiving port for returning troops and 6,000 US personnel passed through the Vicarage Road camp in the three months after D-Day.

The *Derby Daily Telegraph* of Tuesday 27 June told how a wounded Devon soldier was machine-gunned. It stated that while soldiers wounded in Normandy were in a 'duck' (slang for the DUKW amphibious truck) waiting to be transferred to hospital in England, they were deliberately machine-gunned by a German plane.

Private Jack Sadler, aged 18, a member of No.4 Commando, was among them. As he lay helpless in the 'duck,' he received many bullet wounds and he died after reaching hospital. He was the son of William and Margaret Sadler of Paignton, Devon and is buried in Bovey Tracey Cemetery.

At the beginning of July, plans were prepared and presented by Mr A.J.P.B. Alexander for the rebuilding of the centre of Exeter. The plans included the preservation of distinctive characteristics and the building of improved shopping and traffic facilities. It was proposed that Bedford Circus should be expanded and become the centre of an arcaded shopping centre.

On 4 July, a dance was held on Plymouth Hoe to celebrate American Independence Day. Nancy Astor happily danced with American servicemen during the celebrations.

The *Western Morning News* of Thursday 6 July reported that an absentee soldier had been caught stealing from a flat. A 22-year-old soldier, with four previous convictions for shopbreaking, housebreaking and larceny, was sentenced to 18 months' hard labour at the Devon Quarter Sessions after pleading guilty to breaking into a flat in the Strand, Torquay, and stealing a suit of clothes. He was Frederick Watts, of Bristol, who asked for charges of stealing a bicycle and a purse to be taken into consideration.

Passing sentence, the chairman, Sir Archibald Bodkin, said the accused seemed determined to live a dishonest life.

Miss D.K. Belcher, prosecuting, said that the premises were temporarily unoccupied. By opening a kitchen window and removing a lock from the door leading to the kitchen to the rest of the flat, the accused forced an entry.

He was seen later in an air-raid shelter in Torquay, changing from his uniform into civilian clothes and he was arrested and taken to the police station.

Detective Constable Ferris said Watts was the youngest of a family of ten. His parents were not now interested in him

American troops dancing on Plymouth Hoe during 1944. Smeaton's Tower can be seen in the background.

Members of the WVS helping cooks at the Army Cadet camp in Honiton during August 1944. Over 800 cadets were catered for.

because of his associations. He had served a term at Borstal and two prison sentences. Escorted to his unit after last being released from prison in April, he immediately absented himself and committed the offence which he now admitted. It was stated that his army record was bad.

The *Dundee Evening Telegraph* of Friday 4 August reported that an ATS girl at Exeter had been murdered by an American soldier. The trial was set for November.

On 11 August, five members of the Home Guard at Corbyn's Head, Torbay, were killed while carrying out a practice shoot with a 4.7-inch gun. The gun misfired, killing the five men and seriously wounded four others.

The *Western Morning News* of Saturday 19 August carried the story of a rescued bather. It noted that the Mayor of Barnstaple (Alderman Charles F. Dart) and Mr W.T. Buckingham (the chairman of Barnstaple Rural Council) were sponsoring a fund to provide a watch in recognition of the gallantry of a black American soldier who rescued a girl bather from the sea in North Devon.

Major Glenn Miller appeared at the Odeon Cinema in Frankfort Street, Plymouth on 28 August 1944.

The soldier was Private Rudolph Johnson of Jersey who, during his summer-time college vacation, was a lifeguard on an American beach. He was lying on the sand when he heard a shout and seeing the girl bather in difficulties, swam to her assistance and brought her ashore.

In addition to a desire to recognise the courageous action of the soldier, the appeal was also promoted partly to recompense him for the loss of his gold wristlet watch, which he took off and handed to a woman bystander for safety before he went into the water. When he got out, the woman had disappeared with his watch.

Glen Miller band in Plymouth

On 28 August, Major Glenn Miller and his American Band of Allied Expeditionary Force appeared at the Odeon Cinema in Frankfort Street, Plymouth. It was reported that Bing Crosby would also be appearing and large queues started forming at 9pm in readiness for the concert at 10.15pm. Crosby was unable to attend because of other commitments but Glenn Miller appeared and played to a packed house of military and naval personnel (civilians weren't permitted). The police and military police controlled the crowds outside. Miller and his 52-piece orchestra played all the music that he had become famous for. Sergeant Johnny Desmond was the lead vocalist and the Crew Chiefs also appeared on stage. Previous to his appearance, Miller had been given a tour of the city having arrived earlier by plane at Harrowbeer. He gave two other concerts, one at Shapter's Field in Cattedown (where there was a US base) and the other at the US Navy Field Hospital at Manadon.

On 15 December 1944, while flying to Paris from England to give a concert, Glenn Miller's plane, a single-engined UC-64 Norseman, disappeared over the English Channel. No trace of the plane, the crew or Glenn Miller were ever found.

At the beginning of September, the danger of feeding raw swill to farm stock was stressed at a meeting of the Devon Diseases of Animals Committee in Exeter. Captain G. Atkinson, the superintendent veterinary inspector, reported that the origin of the outbreak of foot-and-mouth at Week St Mary was obscure. No fewer than twenty-one instances of the infection had occurred in the country since the beginning of August.

During September, Spooner's in Plymouth, held its first fashion parade since the store was bombed in 1941. The parade took place in the cafe at Drake Circus and included austerity fashions at their best as well as utility models. A number of service girls attended the event keen to be up to date with the latest fashions when they returned to civilian life. Clothes rationing limited purchasing but there was a hope that this would soon be relaxed.

Towards the end of September, it was reported that Italians were assisting in the work of rehabilitating part of the South West which last Christmas had been evacuated in order that American allies could use it as a battle training ground in preparation for D-Day. Two hundred Italian co-operationists worked on the roads and about thirty others were engaged in farm work. The evacuation affected 3,000 people, including 750 households and 180 farms including the villages of East Arlington, Chillington, Blackawton, Sherford, Stokenham, Slapton, Strete and Torcross. The Italians were engaged on hay baling, hedge paring and a variety of other jobs. There were also twenty-five Land Girls and some Irish labour.

It was noted that many sheep and cattle were to be seen grazing on land over which, a few months ago, tank battles were fought and live ammunition whistled past. At East Arlington, the first village to be released, dogs and cats and children were to be seen playing in the lanes and fields which previously rang with the sound of marching men.

Residents were also back in Sherford and Blackawton and people were beginning to trickle back into Chillington which was to be fully released a few days later. Owing to the shortage of labour, caused by the demand from the London area, building repairs were somewhat slower than it was anticipated, but things were moving and the area was being reoccupied.

During October, black grapes fetched £8 a bunch at a gift sale at Bradninch on behalf of the Red Cross Prisoners of War Fund; over £400 was raised by the effort. Outside the Guildhall, livestock, farm and garden produce was auctioned by Mr J. Meadows of Pinhoe. An iced cake, adorned with the Red Cross, raised £10 15s. The receipts for the event totalled £42.

In the second week of October, a flag day was held to raise funds for the Devonshire Nursing Association. The event was held in Exeter where a produce stall was set up in Cathedral Close.

Plymouth's losses counted

The *Western Gazette* of Friday 13 October reported on Plymouth's losses during the bombing of the city. Official figures released of casualties and damage during air raids on Plymouth showed that the city suffered 1,172 civilian deaths and that 3,754 houses had been totally destroyed. Bombs were dropped during 59 of the city's 602 alerts. Injured admitted to hospital totalled 1,092 and slightly injured 2,177, with 7 missing believed killed.

March and April 1941 were the worst months for casualties. In March, 336 people were killed, 285 injured and admitted to hospital and 557 slightly injured. Casualties for April were: killed, 590; injured and admitted to hospital, 438; and slightly injured, 777.

Houses totally destroyed or so badly damaged that they had to be demolished numbered 3,754 and houses seriously damaged, but repairable, 18,398. Houses slightly damaged, including those with broken windows, totalled 49,950.

Forty of Plymouth's churches had been completely destroyed or damaged beyond repair. No hospitals had been entirely destroyed but several had been very badly damaged, including the Royal Eye Infirmary, City Hospital and the Prince of Wales's Hospital. Twenty schools were completely demolished.

On Saturday 14 October, the decision to reduce Civil Defence personnel was made by the Plymouth Emergency Committee. It was also decided to discontinue using certain buildings connected with Civil Defence. With the reduction in risk of an enemy attack, the Ministry of Health reduced by two-thirds the rest care accommodation in the city and the Emergency Committee authorised the closing of all second-line rest centres. A considerable number of vehicles were no longer required and these were returned to the Ministry of Home Security.

The *Daily Mirror* of Tuesday 31 October carried a story about unruly Italians in Tiverton. It was noted that Italian prisoners of war had been posting up crude pictures of Hitler, Mussolini and Mosley on buildings in Tiverton, Devon. Thirty or forty bills, small stylograph copies, were put up in Castle Street and Peter Street. The Italians, who lived in a nearby camp, had also marked Fascist symbols with their fingers on shop windows. Complaints were being made locally of the amount of freedom allowed to the Italians. Soldiers sometimes walked out of dances to prevent trouble.

November proved exceptionally cold in Plymouth with thirteen degrees of frost.

During November, it was reported that an Italian prisoner of war, Bruno Ceolin, 24, had been killed on the Uffculme road when two Americans in a Jeep deliberately ran into him, a woman and her daughter. The woman said that the American driver had previously asked her out but she refused. After knocking down the Italian, the American laughed and said he 'would do her in'. The woman and her daughter were both seriously injured but managed to give evidence at court in Tiverton. The American authorities co-operated fully with the police but the Jeep and its occupants could not be located. A verdict of death by misadventure was recorded.

Murdered by a soldier

The *Western Morning News* of Friday 3 November carried the story of an ATS girl who was murdered by an American soldier:

'Dying declarations by an ATS private, Phyllis Irene Kent, who was stabbed at Rowancroft, an Exeter ATS hostel, last August, were repeated by witnesses who testified before an American Army court-martial, resumed at Exeter yesterday.

Private Kent, aged 25, and the wife of a serving soldier, died in the Royal Devon and Exeter Hospital from a stab wound in the root of the neck. Accused of murdering her is Robert Joseph Himmelmann, a private in the United States Army. He is pleading not guilty.

A dramatic story was told by the first witness called yesterday. She was ATS CSM Elsie M. Glass, who said that at about 9.40pm on August 3, she came out of the sergeants' mess at Rowancroft and saw an American soldier standing at the bottom of the stairs leading to the bedrooms. The soldier was short and fair and she asked him what he was doing. Receiving no coherent answer – only a mutter – she said to him, 'Get out of it'. The soldier took no notice so she repeated to him to 'clear out'. Himmelmann left by the front door and the next witness saw of him was when he was crouched behind a shrubbery in the hostel grounds. She then went to phone for the military police. Afterwards, when talking to other ATS girls, she heard terrifying screams coming from inside the hostel.

'I ran towards the house as fast as I could,' continued CSM Glass. 'As I got to the bend in the drive, I saw the same American soldier running out as hard as he could go. Some of the girls shouted 'Stop him, he has attacked Kent.'

Witness said that she tried to trip the soldier as he passed. Next a Royal Marine closed with him and knocked him over. The American got up, however, and ran quickly into the main road. Here, two policemen joined in the chase and a British soldier also came towards the American. Finally, the American soldier was caught in the grounds of a nearby house.

Asked to identify the soldier, CMS Glass unhesitatingly walked towards the accused and said: 'That is the man here.'

Another member of the ATS, Private Elsworth, said she was just inside the front door of the hostel when she heard terrible screams. An American soldier rushed out and there was something which resembled blood on his forehead. An ATS girl tried to hit him with her handbag.

Witness identified Himmelmann as being the soldier concerned and then went on to say that she saw Private Kent trying to get up the stairs. Kent staggered and fell on her left shoulder. She was screaming and between her screams, she said: 'I am dying.'

When witness asked Kent what had happened, the latter said: 'He came into my room and assaulted me.'

Lance Corporal Pearce said she had just got into bed when she heard screams. She also heard shouts of 'I am bleeding.' She ran downstairs and saw Kent, who was bleeding from a wound in the chest. Kent looked directly at witness and said that an American had assaulted her and that she was bleeding to death. She also said that an American had done it and that she knew she was going to die.'

The hearing was adjourned to the following day.

The *Western Morning News* reported on 6 November that 40 per cent of the 198 fires reported to the NFS in No 19 Fire Force Area, which covered south-west Devon and Cornwall, were down to carelessness. A quarter of these, statistics revealed, were caused by dropped cigarettes and matches while another quarter were due to unattended rubbish fires. Other causes included children playing with matches and electrical faults.

Commander Colonel G. Thomson called for units of the Home Guard of the Plymouth Garrison to stand down at a meeting of 4,000 officers and men on Plymouth Hoe. A march by was accompanied by music from the Royal Marines Band and the men of the Home Guard paraded for the last time.

The *Western Morning News* of Tuesday 19 December reported that the American soldier accused of murder had been found guilty and had been sentenced:

'A private found guilty of the murder of a young woman who was a complete stranger to him was sentenced by a United States Army court-martial near Taunton yesterday.

Private Robert Joseph Himmelmann, 19, of St. Louis, Missouri, was alleged to have stabbed Mrs Phyllis Irene Kent, 25, after he was ordered to leave an ATS hostel at Exeter on the night of August 3.

He was sentenced to dishonourable discharge, to forfeit all pay and allowances, and to life imprisonment with hard labour.'

Lighting orders were rescinded during December and for the first time in years, major streets in Plymouth were allowed reduced lighting. The Royal Cinema's lights shone brightly as they had done pre-war. Masking of car headlamps was no longer compulsory.

The war had made a great number of orphans. At the Christmas pantomime dress rehearsal at the Palace Theatre in Plymouth, 1,200 children were invited. It was

Armed forces proudly marching through Plymouth. Parades boosted morale and many organisations including the Civil Defence, Navy, the Home Guard and the Woman's Voluntary Service all took part. Here, a band plays as it leads the march.

discovered that many of these had no surviving parents and figures confirmed that there were over 1,000 orphans living in Plymouth at the time.

The Lord Mayor's Fund provided money to give all wounded servicemen in Plymouth the best possible Christmas that they could have. In Devonport, the Royal Sailors Rest put on a party, complete with Christmas dinner, for 200. Meanwhile, the St Andrew's Service Canteen gave an afternoon tea for 300 which included cakes and pastries. On Boxing Day, they organised a dance and a buffet. The YMCA in Union Street provided Christmas dinner for 200 which was followed by a party which entertained a further 1,000 guests.

The *Western Morning News* of Thursday 28 December reported that 1944 had been a memorable year in Devon. There had been comparative freedom from enemy action, a removal of the travel ban, a partial lifting of the black-out, restoration of road signs, disbandment of invasion committees, reduction of ARP personnel and standing down of the Home Guard and Fire Guard. They all eased the burden of the worry of war on the home front and encouraged local authorities to think more seriously about post-war planning and problems of peace.

In December, Plymouth bid farewell to the young men from Canada who had spent years in the city carrying out firefighting duties.

CHAPTER 7

1945 – Victory

During January many parts of Devon were cut off by heavy snow and ice. Some villages were unable to get food and supplies. In Oare and Brendon, on the border of Devon and Somerset, supplies were delivered after several days when a party of police officers from Minehead joined a number of soldiers and reached there in a semi-armoured car after receiving an SOS from a special constable living in Oare.

The *Western Morning News* of Tuesday 30 January stated that after many adventures, a party reached Minehead nearly 24 hours after they had set out, having met a search party of more officers from the town, who had been sent out because of the alarm felt at their long absence. Taking stocks of meat, bread, groceries and tobacco, the party made good going until they reached the open road between Porlock and Lynton. Here drifts of six and seven feet of snow were encountered, and at places where the road was impassable and at other points it was not visible, the vehicles drove across the common.

The villages, of which the first, Oare, is about 14 miles from Minehouse, were reached in the late afternoon and, in addition to house-to-house distributions, dumps were also created.

Inspector Linton, in charge of the policemen, said, 'There is no doubt that the people were on their beam ends and their stocks had got very low indeed. It made all our efforts worthwhile to hear people say, "Thank God, you've come."

The mission completed, the party ran into further trouble. They spent three hours trying to get up one hill, and when they eventually managed it by cutting across fields, their petrol ran out because of so much bottom-gear work. After they had replenished their tank at a farm they set off again, but then the front-wheel drive became ineffective, so that no further progress could be made. The vehicle was abandoned and the men then trudged several miles through the snow before linking up miles from Porlock with the search party.

Plymouth and district experienced an even worse snowstorm than previously and soon there were six inches of snow in some districts including Hartley and Crownhill.

The snow followed heavy frost which had entailed careful driving and many narrow escapes for motorists and other users of the road. Pedestrians had become accustomed to walking 'gingerly' on the icy pavements, and although the centre of the city had become practically free from ice, the outlying districts still had a considerable quantity of snow and ice lying on their roads and sidewalks.

Exeter experienced the heaviest fall of snow for many years. In some parts of the city, the depth exceeded a foot. Snow fell in Plymouth covering the floor of St Andrew's Church which had been without a roof for several years.

Towards the end of January, during the final meeting of the County Committee held at the Castle of Exeter, Devon was congratulated, for coming top among all the counties in the recent Red Cross and St John Book Campaign. The High Sheriff Mr B.G. Lampard-Vacheli, who presided, said more than 70,000 volumes had been dispatched, or were in course of dispatch to London. About 10,000 more had been collected in the areas of nine local authorities from whom no figures had come to hand. Forty-eight local authorities had contributed to the success of the drive. Only Lynton Urban, Broadwoodwidger Rural and Crediton Rural had not taken part. Some 3,000 books were coming back to the county for hospital use as a first instalment of their percentage quota. The figure was expected to rise to 5,000.

Captain Alan W. Freeman, the County Organiser, said the local authorities from which no figures had been received were Totnes Borough and Totnes Rural, Dartmouth and Kingswear. Okehampton Rural, Holsworthy Urban, Tavistock Urban and Tavistock Rural, Buckfastleigh Urban and Barnstaple Rural. Altogether in Devonshire, there had been fifty main drives and 282 subsidiary efforts. All those who had taken part in the campaign were warmly thanked.

At the beginning of February, a juvenile court was held at Bideford. Two schoolboy defendants appeared accused of the theft of articles, some belonging to a member of the armed services. They told a remarkable story regarding the reasons for their actions. The two brothers, aged 11 and 8, pleaded guilty to stealing a wooden toy engine, valued at £1, from a store in Bideford Market. The boys, at the time of the alleged offence, were evacuees. One boy, who had been placed on probation before, was placed on probation for three years, and the younger boy was dismissed under the Probation of Offenders' Act.

A boy of 14, who was employed at a local store, was charged with stealing a raincoat belonging to another employee and was fined 30s.

Two 15-year-old schoolboys, one an evacuee, was accused of stealing a parcel of birthday cards belonging to a local store while in the possession of the Southern Railway, as bailees, pleaded not guilty. One boy stated that he took the parcel to 'make the porter run.'

The Bench found the cases proved and the boys asked to have taken into consideration accusations concerning the alleged theft from the Southern Railway Station of a box of torch batteries and a box of apples and oranges, and from a service hut six dozen Very light cartridges, valued at £6 16s. 3d. One of the boys, who had been on probation before was placed on probation for three years, and the other was discharged under the Probation of Offenders Act.

Church vandalized

The *Western Morning News* of Saturday 17 February carried the story of a church damaged by American troops. It stated that aid was coming from America to Blackawton Parish Church, which was wantonly damaged after the area had been used as a battle-training ground by the American Army. The restoration was estimated to cost £1,200.

People found that the vestry window had been smashed and entry gained thereby. The organ had been badly tampered with (it cost £50 to repair) and all the forty-one lamps were taken, as were all the altar ornaments except the cross, the Communion cruets and the wafer box, all the altar linen, the complete set of the burses and veils, the alms bags and the pulpit falls.

When a service of thanksgiving for the homecoming was held, the Bishop referred to the fact that great sacrifices had been made by the people and as the result of the evacuation, the lives of many American soldiers had been saved and had made D-Day possible.

A letter was received from Major A.J. Terrill, the president of the Commonwealth Exploration Corporation and an officer of the California National Guard, of Los Angeles, who wrote:

> I rejoice to note that our American boys obtained their highly valuable training in the Blackawton parish district, but I am grieved to note the acts of sacrilege performed by some person or persons unknown in stealing the vestments and other essential furnishings from the church. I note the appeal of the vicar of Blackawton for £1,200 to replace things that were stolen, more than likely as souvenirs and which have found their way by devious channels to our country.
>
> I intend to lay the whole matter before the Bishop of the Los Angeles Diocese (Protestant), Right Reverend Bertram Stevens, seeking his co-operation in raising the sum called for by the vicar of Blackawton to restore the organ and re-erect the chancel screen and provide the funds to replace all the lamps stolen.
>
> Any wanton destruction would not be condoned by the people of America, especially those who were born citizens of Great Britain and have now become citizens of the US, like myself. The vicar of St Paul's Church (Protestant), in San Diego, California, is also named Stevens, a native of Brixham, Devonshire. I will also enlist his aid.

Sergeant Alfred Gill, of the Tanks Corps, is welcomed home by Colonel G.B. Oerton during March 1945. He was on sick leave from a military hospital and had recently won a Military Medal for gallantry. His home was in Loxhore Mill, North Devon.

By March 1945 the film-going public could buy ice cream again. It had been withdrawn from Gaumont cinemas in 1942.

The *Taunton Courier and Western Advertiser* of Saturday 10 March featured a plea for women potato planters. It stated that in order to prevent a repetition of the potato famine in the following year, volunteers were needed to help farmers in the West Country. The newspaper continued that the response to an appeal for women volunteers to plant potatoes in Devon had been very disappointing. However, there was still time for people to offer their help and it was hoped that many would do so before the first of the Volunteer Agricultural Camps opened.

A camp for women only was to be held at Dreamland Cafe, Okehampton from 8 April to 6 May. This camp had been one the most popular during the previous year. It was situated in the country and could accommodate thirty. It was hoped that the camp would be full for each of the four weeks it was open.

The Dart and South Hams Battalion of the Devon County Cadet Force passing the saluting base at Totnes during March 1945. The salute was taken by Colonel A.J.H. Sloggett DSO, who was the County Commandant.

The First Lord of the Admiralty, A.V. Alexander, visited Plymouth during March to open the new NAAFI Club in Lockyer Street. The site had previously housed the Royal Hotel.

In early April, the Allies pushed into Italy and western Germany while the Soviet and Polish forces stormed Berlin at the end of the month.

Left: Colonel A.J.H. Sloggett, the County Commandant, inspecting the smallest member of the 6th Dart and South Hams Battalion of the Devon County Cadet Force in March 1945. He told the colonel that he hoped to be a marine when he left the cadets.

Right: A US wedding in Devon. Lieutenant E. Safir and Lieutenant Nurse A. Dittmar married at the Congregational Church at Newton Abbot during April 1945.

The *Western Morning News* of Monday 16 April told of the surrender of Germans to a Devon officer. The article told how German captors surrendered to their captives and was related to a *Western Morning News* representative by Captain P. Griffin, the son of Mr N.B. Griffin, of Newstead House, Paignton, who was serving with a medical unit of the 1st Airborne Division when captured at Arnhem.

'It was an exciting time when we learnt that American armour was about five miles away from our camp,' he said. 'The Germans moved all the prisoners except those unable to walk and next morning we heard firing. The German guards came and hid in our air raid shelters and their commandant practically surrendered to the Allied camp commandant. Unfortunately, the tanks went right past and an anxious time followed.'

'Next day,' continued Captain Griffin, 'the German commander telephoned to a village about a mile away and got a message to an American command post, as a result of which the Americans sent jeeps and rescued us.'

Captain Griffin said that the main point of his experience was that the Red Cross was an absolute godsend. He added that now the Germans knew the war was lost the whole tone of this treatment had changed considerably and they were a little more human. In all the cases he came across of medical treatment of prisoners by Germans, it had been very good. He could honestly say that.

On 28 April Benito Mussolini was killed by Italian partisans. German forces surrendered in Italy on the following day. On 30 April Adolf Hitler committed suicide in his bunker in Berlin. The news reached Devon two days later. Many people thought that the story was a hoax. On the same day, the air-raid warning system ceased in Plymouth.

A lion tamer entertaining the public at Paignton Zoo in April 1945.

With the capture of the Reichstag the military defeat of Nazi Germany was inevitable. Germany surrendered unconditionally on 7 May to much jubilation all over the world.

VE Day Celebrations
The *Western Morning News* of Monday 7 May reported on the proposed VE celebrations in Plymouth. Service and civic officials in Plymouth were busily engaged during the weekend completing the arrangements for VE Day. On the night of VE Day, dance music was to be broadcast on the Hoe until midnight.

The route for the Thanksgiving Sunday parade of British and Allied Services, Civil Defence Services, and youth organisations was announced on the previous Saturday.

They were told to assemble at Beaumont Road at 2.30pm and march through Ebrington Street, Drake Circus, Old Town Street and Bedford Street, where the Lord Mayor (Alderman H.G. Mason) would take the salute. At George Street, Union Street, Stonehouse Bridge, Kings Road, Paradise Road and Fore Street, Commander-in-Chief Plymouth (Admiral Sir Ralph Leatham) would take the salute and at Marlborough Street, the parade would disperse. Transport arrangements during victory celebrations were to be operated as normally as possible. The transport manager (Mr C. Jackson) stated that as soon as the 'All Clear' hooters were sounded, the workmen's buses would leave the depot half an hour later. For

VE day celebrations in Plymouth. A large crowd has gathered around the Guildhall to listen to dignitaries and members of the armed forces. The church bells rang out all over the city; previously they had been banned except to announce an enemy invasion.

Children celebrate Victory in Europe. Here they wave flags around a bonfire. Up and down the country, and around the world, parties were held to celebrate VE day. There was much merriment along with singing and dancing. On 7 May 1945, Germany surrendered and 8 May 1945 was declared as VE Day.

those who had to work on the two-day holiday, the workmen's services would be operated as far as possible; it was hoped to run a fairly full general service but this entirely depended upon the available staff. All cinemas and the Palace Theatre would be open throughout the celebrations, but there was no extension of hours at public houses etc.

Victory in Europe Day was on 8 May and the official ceasefire ended a minute after midnight on 9 May. Huge celebrations took place all over Devon with every city, town and village organising its own parades and street parties with endless flags and bunting as well as bonfires and firework displays. Most bonfires featured an effigy of Hitler on top. For the first time since the beginning of the war, shops once more lit up their windows. Bonfires were lit on Plymouth Hoe and thousands turned up to celebrate including many servicemen as well as civilians.

The Admiralty lifted lighting restrictions in coastal areas on 11 May, normal street lighting returned and traffic lights no longer had to be masked.

German officers arrive from the Channel Islands

The *Western Morning News* of Monday 14 May carried a story under the headline NAZI CHIEFS AT PLYMOUTH. It noted that a British destroyer had glided into

Smiling faces at a VE Day party in Mount Gould, Plymouth.

Plymouth harbour late on the previous Saturday night with two German officers of high rank as prisoners of war. They were Vice Admiral Huffmeier, commander of the German naval forces in the Channel Islands, and Major General Wolfe commanding the German army of occupation in the islands.

The captured German Submarine, U-1023 *which was surrendered on 10 May 1945.*

The officers, with a batman each, were transferred to the Royal Citadel and remained there overnight.

Shortly before 9.30am on the Sunday, the Garrison Commander (Colonel G. Thompson), accompanied by Captain C.F. Nicholas, arrived at the Royal Citadel to supervise the departure of the prisoners. Three military tenders were waiting and a few minutes before their departure, a youthful German soldier brought out his general's luggage and placed it in one of the tenders. He was closely guarded by a Royal Artillery man with a rifle.

Immediately afterwards, a German Navy man, carefully guarded, came out with Admiral Huffmeier's luggage and placed it in the first tender. In the meantime, British orderlies were handing out haversack rations for the Germans and their officer escort, Major Hilditch, of the Royal Citadel, and a lieutenant and the Royal Artillerymen who accompanied the German batman. What appeared to be Cornish pasties were contained in some of the paper bags prepared for the Germans.

A tall, clean-shaven, typical German naval officer of about 50, Admiral Huffmeier, in long blue coat with light purple lapels and Iron Cross, emerged from the officers' mess and approached the Garrison commander and stood smartly to attention. Following closely after the German admiral came General Wolff in faded field grey uniform with bright red lapels, with top boots and spurs, a man of about 50. He stood a few paces behind Admiral Huffmeier. After the Garrison Commander had explained the procedure to him, Admiral Huffmeier said, 'Will you tell your officers and men I am very grateful for the arrangements that have been made for us.'

The German admiral took the front seat alongside a Devon ATS driver, while Major Hilditch occupied a seat in the rear of the transport. The second car was occupied by the German general, sitting in front by the girl driver, and his escort, a lieutenant of the Royal artillery, sat behind. The third car was occupied by the escort and the batman with the baggage.

The guard at the Royal Citadel sprang to attention as the tenders, headed by the Garrison commander's car, swept through the archway en route for Friary Station, where the Garrison commander and Captain Nicholas supervised the departure of the prisoners by the 10am train for Waterloo. The German officers, who looked well-fed, stepped into a first-class compartment, while their batmen and escorts occupied the adjacent third-class compartment. The German officers, looking calm and indifferent, occupied the far corner seats.

Open-air services were held at Devonport Park and within the shell of St Andrew's Church on 13 May. At St Jude's, a thanksgiving parade was marshalled by Major Wattenbach, the Brigade Major of Plymouth Garrison.

Two Naval destroyers sailed into Plymouth Sound on the evening of 17 May with six captured German minesweepers and two patrol craft. The enemy vessels were boarded at Cawsand by two senior naval officers and a contingent of Royal Marines who accepted the surrender of the German commander. As the vessels arrived in the Sound, huge crowds gathered to watch before the ships were taken to Millbay Docks and the crew were taken to the Royal Citadel.

The *Western Morning News* of Tuesday 22 May reported on the round up of Nazis by Devon troops. It noted that after being the spearhead of the attack from the beaches of Normandy to the final surrender of the German armed services in the North West, the battalion of the Devonshire Regiment found that victory in Europe still meant plenty of hard work.

Together with the rest of the Seventh Armoured Division (The Desert Rats), the Devons rounded up the broken and weary Wehrmacht divisions as they straggled down the frontier roads from Denmark. They were put into specially-prepared concentration areas. Some 70,000 German servicemen were shepherded in three days. The battalion occupied a strategic town on the main frontier road and found out that it had other problems on its hands apart from the defeated enemy. Liberated slave workers including Russians, Poles, Czechs and French all crowded in as soon as news of their freedom reached them. The motley international crowd had to be sorted out, fed, clothed and even bathed. One officer remarked, 'We need to be expert linguists to try and get some order. It is a real headache but we are making the Germans do a lot of the hard work. They have to lift their own land-mines and booby-traps and, under the direction of the Allied Military Government officials, administer and feed these thousands of prisoners, who arrive in a never-ending stream.'

Private Kenneth Rattenbury. whose home was at 24 Third Avenue, Teignmouth, Devon, spoke to the *Western Morning News* as he stood guard on a bridge over a canal in brilliant sunshine.

'This is the queerest job I've ever had,' he commented. 'I don't know whether I'm a private or a general, for these Jerries are so anxious to do the right thing and keep out of trouble that they all salute me, and proper fashion, too; none of the 'Heil Hitler' stuff. Nearly all the troops are completely subdued and beaten and march through the town here with heads down as they are ashamed to be seen by their own people. Occasionally they are arrogant, like the Marines who came singing: 'We are marching on to England.' We soon shut them up.

We have had quite a lot of SS men through. There was one lorry-load who said they had thrown their arms away but when we searched them we found that each one had got an automatic pistol hidden away. It seems that the SS are hated by the Wehrmacht and were scared of getting a rough handling from them when they found themselves the minority and no Hitler to go and cry to. Another SS bunch each had a girl with them. They said they were their secretaries and typists. We soon stopped that fraternization, too.'

The Lord Mayor of London, Sir Frank Alexander, officially opened the Plymouth Royal Merchant Navy's Week on 26 May. The event took place at the Abbey Hall and its aim was to raise £15,000.

Also, on 26 May, a German U-boat arrived at Plymouth. It had been captured after its commander had surrendered at Portland. The U-boat was being displayed in various ports to raise money for King George's Fund for Sailors.

In June, it was announced that the total raised during the RSPCA flag day in Combe Martin was £12 0s. 3d.

Private Peter Sanders, RAMC, the third son of Mrs and the late Councillor J.H. Sanders of Dudley House, Combe Martin, received a hearty welcome by the Welcome Home Committee in Combe Martin, after having been a prisoner of war for three years. He was captured in Tobruk.

A farewell party was given to the evacuee children at Combe Martin at the beginning of June. Tea was served by Mrs W.J. Delve and her committee. The scholars were entertained to maypole and folk dancing by children from the junior school, who had been trained by Miss Sanders. This was followed by sports events arranged by Mr Hearn. At the conclusion of the races, a netball match took place between two teams composed of the GTC and the Modern Secondary School. A football match was played between the London Boys and the Devon Boys, the result being 1 – 1. A return match was played on the following Monday evening, when the Devonians were successful by 5 goals to 2.

A letter from a Devon soldier serving overseas appeared in the *Western Times* of Friday 1 June:

At long last the war in Europe is finally over. The 'Cease Fire' when it was ordered in North West Germany sounded for the third time in this war for me and a large proportion of the men serving with me in this regiment. The other two occasions were in Iraq and Syria in 1941. The general comment was 'Thank

Heaven it's all over at last; most of us having a feeling of relief, rather than any great excitement.'

Now that it's all over, I would like to say how much I have appreciated the *Western Times* during practically the whole war. Since February, 1940, when I went to the Middle East, it has provided me with many pleasant hours in some of the most outlandish places. I have enjoyed its columns in Palestine, Syria, Iraq, Cyprus, Egypt and the Western Desert, Italy and now, finally, Germany, the farmyard of what we have been doing our bit to crush.

During my stay in the Middle East, our role consisted, at times, of fairly long spells of internal security. The old paper was a great source of comfort during these periods, the stories of Jan Stewer often relieving a very strained atmosphere. Men from all parts of England, as well as a few from Scotland, used to find these stories equally as amusing as I did.

I would like to include a special word of thanks to my mother, Mrs T. Vanstone, of Langtree, who has sent me the paper with such regularity. Never a week did she miss, although at one time, one or two copies didn't get through as the result of enemy action. As you can probably imagine, news from home was always welcome and eagerly looked for. The local paper was always just as welcome as, although letters contain the majority of all that's happening, the paper covers a much wider area and keeps one in touch with the outlying districts.

Since I went overseas in February, 1940, and between then and October, 1944 (when I returned to England for a short stay), I travelled several thousand miles, perhaps over a million. I kept no record, in all types of vehicles. Since coming to North-West Europe early last March, I've added another thousand or two to the grand total and my biggest hope is that I do not have to do so very many more before I start on my return journey to Devon, and especially Langtree, where I have so many good friends, both old and young. May I take this opportunity to say 'Thank you very much' to all of them for the many kindnesses they showed me. May they have every prosperity and good health in the new peace.

To those that have relatives overseas may I say: 'Be of good cheer. The time of your reunion is not far away.'

To all my old school pals may I say 'Chins up and keep smiling wherever you are.' To those in the Far East: 'Well done so far. We've finished this part of the war and I'm sure it won't be long before we hear that you've done the same out there.'

All members of the forces from Langtree join me in saying thank you very much to the hard-working members of the village comforts committee. I'll conclude by wishing you and all the staff of the good old *Western Times,* 'All the very best in the coming years of peace.' Keep the old paper rolling off the press. I'll be reading it with my carpet slippers on soon (I hope).

My best wishes to all my friends and relatives in Devon. I'll be seeing you soon.'

Dairymaids taking part in a competition at Willtown Farm, Lifton, where Lifton and Tavistock Young Farmers' Clubs held stock-judging and milking competitions in June 1945.

Life was slowly returning to normal. On 13 June pleasure cruises resumed in Plymouth after being suspended at the beginning of the war. The first liner to call at Plymouth for five and a half years, *Drina*, arrived on the 19 June. The vessel had travelled from Argentina and on board were twenty-five passengers and 7,000 tons of meat destined for British troops serving in Germany.

HMAS *Australia* arrived at Devonport on 1 July. The flagship of the Australian Royal Navy was taken to the Dockyard for a refit and repair. She had been hit at the Battle of Leyte during October 1944 by a Japanese bomber. While in the city, the crew of 700 were entertained at dances, cinemas and the theatre.

The US troops celebrating Independence Day on 4 July 1945 at Raglan Barracks in Devonport. Here, the men listen to a speech from the garrison commander.

The *Western Morning News* of Tuesday 10 July carried a story under the headline DEVONS IN BURMA. It mentioned that Captain H.J.J. Herring, of Highlands, Crownhill, Plymouth, was on leave in the city after service with the Devonshire Regiment in the Imphal and Burma campaigns. He was impressed by the manner in which the devastated areas of Plymouth were being cleaned up and expressed the hope that the process of reconstruction will be as speedily carried through as conditions permit.

He asked the *Western Morning News* to record the appreciation of his battalion of the splendid work being done by the women of Devon who were knitting socks and other comforts for them. Captain Herring emphasised, as his commanding officer had already done, that the cigarettes, etc sent from home made all the difference.

The local organizer of the fund which was instrumental in collecting cigarettes had received several letters which confirmed that whereas cigarettes sent privately frequently fail to reach their destination, those dispatched in bulk through the Comforts Fund were arriving safely.

A donation to the fund was received from the parents of an officer of the regiment who lost his life in France after service in the Mediterranean theatre. Among recent staff collections was a contribution from Messrs Underhill (Plymouth), Ltd, who also supplied publicity matter gratuitously.

At Oreston, Sergeant F. Ducker was welcomed home in the summer of 1945 after his release from a prisoner of war camp.

During July, a hearing at Plympton Magistrates' Court heard further cases arising out of the torpedoing of the Belgian steamer *Persier* in the Channel during the previous February. Foodstuffs and soap had been washed up on the beaches around Salcombe and Bigbury and six people from the Bigbury area were summoned for being in possession of wreckage and failing to deliver it to the Receiver of Wreck. The defendants pleaded not guilty.

The alleged circumstances were that on 11 February, the Belgian steamer *Persier*, bound from Cardiff to Antwerp, was sunk in the Channel when loaded with some 8,000 tons of foodstuffs etc for Belgium. On the following day, wreckage began to be washed ashore on the beaches from Stoke Point to Bolt Head.

Captain W.R. Beer, who represented the defendants, submitted that there was no case to answer. It was the duty of the Receiver of Wreck to proceed to the place where the wreckage was stranded, but it was impossible for anyone to know who the Receiver of Wreck was unless they saw the notices which were supposed to have been put up. One of the accused had been told by an official that he could take away any loose soap or any loose tins. 'There is not the slightest doubt in my opinion that that official told these people they could do that. There is only one course to adopt, and that is to dismiss this charges,' he added.

After a short retirement, the Chairman (Mr W.J. Swords), who sat with Mrs E.M. Choake and Mr D.H. Gill, said the case would be dismissed. Captain Beer asked for costs, which were refused.

Double summer time came to an end on 14 July and the clocks were put back an hour. Double Summer Time had been introduced earlier in the war to boost productivity and to ensure that munitions workers didn't have to travel home in the dark.

President Truman meeting King George VI on board HMS Renown *in Plymouth Sound on 2 August 1945. The battleship USS* Augusta *can be seen in the background.*

Two female football teams, representing the ATS and Tavistock, played a match at Tavistock in connection with the Welcome Home Week carnival in August 1945.

On 2 August King George VI met the President of the United States on board HMS *Renown* while the vessel was in Plymouth Sound. Harry S. Truman had become President after the sudden death of Franklin D. Roosevelt in April.

The United States Army Air Forces dropped an atomic bomb on Hiroshima, Japan on 6 August, which killed 80,000 people instantly. Nagasaki was bombed three days later, ultimately bringing the war in Japan to an end.

On 14 August the new Prime Minister, Clement Attlee, announced the surrender of Japan. All over Devon, places of work were closed for two days during the VJ celebrations.

In Plymouth on 15 August VJ Day was celebrated by bonfires on Plymouth Hoe and at Devonport Park and Central Park. Almost 60,000 people gathered to watch the event on the Hoe.

Huge crowds gathered at Dawlish and a bonfire was lit on the main beach and fireworks were set off. People danced on the lawns to the early hours. Meanwhile, in Totnes, there was a parade, a thanksgiving service and street parties. The celebrations were much the same all over Devon.

On 2 September, the Japanese surrender documents were signed on board the American battleship USS *Missouri* which marked the official end of the Second World War.

With the war at an end, people celebrated but remembered their lost loved ones who had been killed on the battlefield or in the streets and homes of British towns and cities. No family was untouched by the war. Food remained rationed but people were now entitled to an extra half-ounce of tea. However, rationing continued until 1954 and it was a long time before Great Britain recovered from its effects. The long process of rebuilding and returning to normal took place. Many cities, such as Plymouth, were almost completely rebuilt and a way of life was lost forever.

Acknowledgements

Thanks to Tina Cole, Alan Tait, Ellen Tait and Tilly Barker. Thanks also to the helpful and friendly team at Pen and Sword, including Roni Wilkinson, Matt Jones, Jon Wilkinson, Irene Moore, Diane Wordsworth, Katie Eaton, Laura Lawton, Jodie Butterwood, Tara Moran and Lisa Goose.

Bibliography

Books

Devon at War 1938 – 1945 by Gerald Wasley (Devon Books 1994)

It Came to Our Door: Plymouth in World War II – a Journalist's Eye Witness Account by H.P. Twyford and Chris Robinson (Pen & Ink Publishing 2005)

Plymouth–A City at War 1914-45 by John Van Der Kiste (The History Press 2014)

Plymouth as Time Draws on by Chris Robinson (Pen & Ink Publishing 1985)

Plymouth at War: A Pictorial Account, 1939-45 by Keith Scrivener (Archive Publications *Evening Herald* 1989)

Plymouth at War from Old Photographs by Derek Tait (Amberley 2012)

Plymouth at War (Images of England) by Derek Tait (History Press 2006)

Plymouth at War Through Time by Derek Tait (Amberley 2011)

Plymouth Blitz by Frank Wintle (Bossiney 1985)

Plymouth Blitz –The Story of the Raids by H.P. Twyford (*Western Morning News* 1947)

Plymouth in the Forties and Fifties by Chris Robinson (Pen & Ink Publishing 2011)

Put That Light Out! by Mike Brown (Sutton Publishing 1999)

The Blitz of Plymouth 1940–1944 by Arthur Clamp (PDS Printers 1981)

Newspapers

Daily Mirror
Derby Daily Telegraph
Dundee Evening Telegraph
Express and Echo
Exeter and Plymouth Gazette
Gloucestershire Echo
London Gazette
North Devon Journal
Taunton Courier and Western Advertiser
Western Gazette
Western Independent
Western Morning News
Western Times
Yorkshire Evening Post

Index

Abercrombie, Professor Patrick, 167
Abyssinian War, 43
Achilles, 26, 34
Admiralty, 22, 31, 36, 56, 134, 185, 188
Agriculture Committee, 34
Aid-to-China Fund, 165
Air Raid Precautions Officer, 13
Air-raid sirens, 13
Air Training Corps, 64, 144
Ajax, HMS, 26, 31, 34, 36
Alhambra Theatre, 49, 76
Aliens, 18–19, 41
Allied invasion, 171, 173
Allotment holders, 40
America, 84, 111, 116, 119, 173, 183–4
American Committee for Air Raid
    Relief, 138
American Naval Construction
    Battalion, 151
American Red Cross, 144, 153, 159
Anderson shelters, 38
Animal Rescue Squad, 79
Appledore, 66, 134, 151–2
Arlington House, Teignmouth, 24
Army Blood Transfusion Service, 82
ARP wardens, 13
Astor Club, 119
Astor, Lady, 20, 29, 66, 77–8, 80, 84, 87,
    89, 91, 94, 99–101, 118–19, 122, 132,
    154, 175
Astor, Lord, 20, 40, 66, 76, 84, 90, 95,
    100, 154, 156, 167
Astor, Lord and Lady, 20, 66, 91,
    144, 153
Atlee, Clement, 197
Austrians, 10
Auxiliary Fire Service, 51, 84, 130
Auxiliary Messenger Service, 144
Axminster, 21

Baden-Powell, Lady, 141–2
Barbican, 57, 59
Barnstaple, 9, 11, 20, 29, 34, 38, 41,
    57, 59, 82, 89, 100, 103, 107, 111,
    116–17, 119, 135, 148, 152, 158,
    176, 183
Barnstaple Rural Council, 128, 163
Barrage balloon, 7–8, 13, 39, 126
Battle of Britain, 31, 46, 48, 52, 55,
    129, 171
Battle of the River Plate, 26, 34, 36
BBC, 8, 100, 171
Berlin Wintergarten, 49
Bideford Borough Magistrates, 51, 121
Birmingham, 16, 50, 55
Black-out, 8, 13, 19, 22, 29–30, 52, 122,
    133, 135, 152, 181
Blitz, 52, 59–60, 68, 70, 72, 75, 78–9,
    81, 86–7, 91–2, 94, 98, 104–106,
    111–14, 118, 123, 135, 146, 149,
    162, 166–7
Blitz of London, 52
Board of Trade, 133, 161
Bomb disposal squad, 61, 77, 82, 123
Bowden Hall, 96–7
Brent Station, 64
Brighton Belle, 42
Bristol, 56, 64–6, 112–13, 115, 146, 175
Britannia, HMS, 152
British Empire Medal, 106
British Expeditionary Force, 42
British Legion, 13–14, 108, 156, 157
British Red Cross, 46, 113
Brixham, 48, 50, 173, 184
Buckland Monachorum, 28
Burrator Reservoir, 151

Campbell, Colin, 13, 47, 91, 155
Canadian firefighters, 131, 147

Candles, 16, 30
Carlile Davis, S., 9
Castle Street Congregational Rooms, 9
Chamberlain, Neville, 8, 40
Channel Islands, 44, 47, 135, 188–9
Chessington, 51
Christmas, 19, 29–30, 57, 59–60, 114, 116–17, 119, 135, 158, 177, 180–1
Churchill, Winston, 36, 40, 43–4, 46, 50, 89, 99, 100, 116
Church of England Waifs and Strays' Society, 124
City Air Raid Relief Fund, 161
City of Benares, SS, 52
Civil Defence, 15, 22–3, 39, 67, 69, 79, 84, 91, 97, 112–13, 117, 120, 124, 140, 151, 154–5, 164, 166, 178, 181, 187
Clements, John, 16
Combined Operations Experimental Establishment, 152
Conscientious objectors, 17, 146
Control of Noises (Defence) Order, 30
Convoy SC19, 63
Cornwall, 9, 15, 24–5, 45–6, 104, 114, 123, 125, 142, 144, 147, 156, 161, 180
County Warships Weeks Championship, 114
Courageous, HMS, 14, 37
Coward, Noël, 87, 101
Coxside, 63
Crimean War, 111
Cullompton's Assembly Rooms, 20

Dambusters, 151
Dartmoor, 23, 34, 50, 108, 121, 151
Dartmoor Prison, 23
Dartmouth, 34, 100, 116, 123, 129, 134–40, 152, 165, 173, 183
Dartmouth Naval College, 100
Dartmouth Young Fellowship, 116
Davey, Michael, 21–2
Dawlish Flag Day, 154

D-Day, 151, 154, 157, 159–60, 165, 173–5, 177, 184
Defence Corps Company, 13
Denmark, 36, 191
Derry's Clock, 67, 74
Devon Agricultural Association, 22
Devon Air Squadron Fund, 103
Devon and Cornwall Female Orphanage, 24–5
Devon Assize, 135
Devon Belle, 42
Devon Cider, 166
Devon Constabulary, 10
Devon County Education Authorities, 60
Devon County Show, 22
Devon County War Agricultural Executive Committee, 15
Devonia, 42
Devonport, 13–14, 31, 34, 47–50, 55, 62, 66, 69, 76, 98–9, 105, 117, 126, 142–3, 151, 157, 166, 173, 181, 191, 194, 197
Devonshire Regiment, 140, 151, 191, 195
Dig for Victory, 32
Distinguished Flying Cross (DFC), 117, 164
Dockyard, 13, 52, 76, 124, 126, 173, 194
Drake Street War Aid Supply Depot, 15
Drewsteignton, 33
Duke of Cornwall Hotel, 30
Duke of Kent, 100
Dunkirk, 42, 44–5, 129, 170–1

E-boats, 140, 165
Earl Fortescue, 105
East Devon, 22, 34, 117, 151
Edinburgh Road Camp, 166
Edwards, Brigadier General W.F.S., 13
Eisenhower, General Dwight, 144, 153
Emergency Committee, 47, 91, 167, 178

Emergency Powers (Defence) Regulations, 13
Emergency War budget, 14
Empty Stocking Fund, 19, 135
Exercise Tiger, 165
Exeter, 9–11, 13, 16, 23, 30, 37, 39, 43–4, 46, 50, 56, 59–61, 64, 103, 106, 108, 110–12, 121–5, 131, 135–6, 140–1, 144, 146–7, 151, 153–4, 156, 158, 161, 165, 175–80, 182
Exeter British Legion Band, 108
Exeter Cathedral, 135
Exeter City Education Committee, 60
Exeter City Police, 10, 61, 144
Exeter, HMS, 26, 28, 34, 36–7
Exeter Prison, 151
Exeter Rotary Club, 103, 111
Exmouth, 10, 34, 40, 60, 82, 116, 119, 125, 131, 140–1, 143, 154, 156–7
Exmouth Dock, 34
Exmouth Food Control Committee, 40
Exmouth Rugby Football Club, 140
Exmouth Stamp Club, 143
Europe, 7, 47, 144, 153, 165, 174, 188, 191–3
Evacuees, 10–11, 15, 20, 29, 38, 46, 52, 57, 59–60, 65, 113, 135, 151, 183

Falkland Islands, 34, 36
Fighter Command, 146
Fire-watching, 60
First World War, 8, 16
Fisher, Sir Warren, 10
Flag Day, 46, 103–104, 125, 128, 154, 165, 178, 192
Fleet Air Arm, 120
Focke-Wulf 190, 136, 140, 147
Food Office, 31, 38, 60, 134
Foreland Point, 31
Four Feathers, 16
France, 7, 42–6, 82, 104, 115, 169–70, 173–4, 195
Free French Naval Forces, 140

Galmpton, 48
Gas mask, 8, 10–11, 13, 40–2, 54
George Cross, 52–3
German Embassy, 9
Germany, 7, 14, 31, 42, 48–9, 52, 82, 104, 111, 116, 141–2, 162, 185, 187–8, 192–4
Girl Guides, 141–2
Girls' Training Corps, 124
Glen Avon, 42
Graf Spee, 26, 28, 31, 34, 37
Great Britain, 7, 31, 42–3, 49, 138, 151, 184, 197
Great Panjandrum, 152
Guildhall Square, 30, 66

Hamoaze House, 26, 173
Harrowbeer, 105, 177
Harstad, HMS, 140
Heinkel III, 65
Heygate Street School, Walworth, 22
Highway code, 148
Hitler, Adolf, 7, 26, 28, 47–9, 52, 178, 186, 188, 192
Holberton, 57
Home Guard, 41, 50–2, 97, 104, 107–108, 119, 126, 128, 131, 136, 140, 147–8, 164, 166, 176, 180–1
Home Sweet Home Terrace, 48
Hore-Belisha, Leslie, 99, 117
Hospital Week, 111
House of Commons, 43, 46, 119
Hull, Lady, 22

ID cards, 10, 52, 134, 173
Ilfracombe, 31, 38, 42, 52, 63, 65, 82, 105, 107, 114, 127, 146, 151, 166
Ilfracombe Evacuation Committee, 65
Ilfracombe's War Weapons Week, 82
Infantry Divisions, 134
Instow beach, 152
Internment camps, 18
Inverdargle, 31

Italians, 43, 177–8
Ivybridge, 111

Jam ration, 107
Japan, 116, 128, 148, 194, 197
Jewish community, 19
Jewish refugees, 18
Johnston Terrace School, 105

Kennedy, Joseph, 9
Keyham, 52–3, 66, 105
King George VI, 26, 52, 66, 123, 196–7
Kingsbridge Estuary, 34
King's Squad of Royal Marines, 141

Lady Mayoress of Plymouth, 19,
    91, 172
Laira, 48, 81, 105, 151, 173
Lancastria, RMS, 44
Land Army, 11–12, 26, 34–5, 104, 109,
    111, 148, 161
Landing Ship Tanks, 165
La Pallice, 44
Last Post, 36
Launceston, 9, 108–109
Leicester Harmsworth House, 19
Le Part Bleu, 52
Lever Brothers Ltd, 113
Lifebuoy Emergency Bath Unit, 113
Liverpool, 17, 42, 59, 75, 114
Local Defence Volunteers, 41
Logan, Major F.R., 9
London, 7, 9, 11, 20–2, 29, 32, 36–7,
    45–6, 51–54, 57, 59–60, 83, 103, 110,
    112, 114, 120–1, 167, 177, 183, 192
Lord Hailsham, HMS, 140
Lord Mayor's Fund, 181
Lord Mayor's Hut Buffet, 86
Luftwaffe, 44, 48, 52, 55, 59, 68, 104,
    115, 119, 147
Lundy Island, 66
Lusitania, RMS, 44
Lyme Bay, 165
Lynmouth, 31

Marks and Spencers, 149
Mayor of Exeter's Air Raid Distress
    Fund, 124
Merchant Navy, 117, 165, 192
Millbay Docks, 26, 191
Miller, Glenn, 176–7
Minehead, 31, 133, 182
Minehead and District Co-operative
    Society, 133
Ministry of Food, 38, 55, 107,
Ministry of Health, 47, 178
Ministry of Information, 112, 116
Moldavia, 140
Monkton Wyld, 22
Montgomery, General, 171
Moretonhampstead Farmers' Union, 114
Mosley, Oswald, 38, 178
Mount Batten, 56, 173
Mount Edgcumbe, 102
Mount Wise, 124
Mutley, 8, 53, 59, 62, 64, 67, 70,
    95, 146

National Defence Company, 14
National Farmers' Union, 161
National Fire Service, 81, 84
National Jewish Women's
    Committee, 19
National Registration Act, 10
National Services Act, 8
Navy, 9, 22, 34, 36, 42, 54, 66–7,
    80–1, 85, 87, 91–3, 98, 112, 117, 134,
    143, 155, 165, 167, 177, 181, 190,
    192, 194
Navy salvage force, 87
Nazi party, 7, 18
Newton Abbot, 22, 50, 106, 128, 132,
    152, 185
New Year, 30, 57, 59–60, 117, 163
Nightingale, Florence, 111
Normandy, 171–5, 191
North Africa, 38, 170–1
North Devon Blood Transfusion
    Week, 89

North Devon Infirmary, 29, 111, 116, 132
North Road Station, 8, 49, 125
North West Regional Commissioner, 10

Octagon Youth Club, 161
Okehampton, 34, 56, 106, 109, 136, 170, 183, 185
Okehampton Fire Brigade, 106
Omaha, 160, 173
Operation Duck, 159
Operation Neptune, 173
Operation Overlord, 151, 173
Operation Sea Lion, 49
Order of the British Empire, 106
Order of St John, 113
Oreston, 57–8, 195
Orphans, 20, 180–1

Paignton, 18, 51, 106, 122, 129, 140, 156, 175, 186
Paper Controller, 38
Parcels for the Troops, 57
Paris, 42, 177
PDSA, 79
Pearl Harbor, 116
Petrol rationing, 13–14
Pinhoe, 22, 178
Plymouth, 7–11, 13–15, 17–21, 23, 25–31, 33–40, 42–57, 59–68, 70–78, 81–3, 86–101, 103–106, 110–14, 118–27, 129–40, 142–50, 151–55, 157–62, 165–78, 180–2, 185–9, 191–2, 194–7
Plymouth Albion, 14
Plymouth Argyle, 96
Plymouth City Council, 21, 81, 119
Plymouth Co-operative Society, 60, 71
Plymouth's Emergency Committee, 47
Plymouth Employment Exchange, 18
Plymouth Food Control Committee, 55
Plymouth Hoe, 33, 39, 62, 67, 78, 101, 103, 105, 126, 175, 180, 188, 197
Plymouth School of Art, 17

Plymouth Sound, 34, 44, 191, 196–7
Poland, 7, 163
Pophams, 60, 94
President Warfield, USS, 151
Prisoners of War Fund, 135, 143, 154, 178
Public Assistance Institute, 116

Queen Elizabeth, 66, 123, 137
Queen's Messengers Convoy, 137–8

Rabbits Order, 118
Racism, 129
RAF, 48, 50–2, 56, 64, 91, 103–105, 114, 117, 124–5, 127
Raleigh, HMS, 76, 90
Ration books, 21, 31, 60
Rationing, 13–14, 31, 34, 37–8, 134, 145, 158, 160, 177, 197
Red Cross Agricultural Fund, 120
Repulse, HMS, 116
Reserved occupations, 17
Richardson, Ralph, 16
River Taw, 34
River Thames, 31
River Torridge, 151
RM Barracks Stonehouse, 141
Roosevelt, President, 116, 197
Royal Air Force Volunteer Reserve, 117
Royal Albert Hospital, 48
Royal Armoured Corps, 27, 108
Royal Auxiliary of Civil Nursing Reserve, 17
Royal Devon and Exeter Hospital, 103, 125, 140, 154, 161, 179
Royal Eye Infirmary, 62, 64, 178
Royal Marines, 9, 37, 107, 141, 180, 191
Royal Naval Barracks, 26, 124
Royal Naval Engineering College, 26
Royal Navy, 9, 34, 66, 80, 91, 117, 194
Royal Oak, HMS, 21
Royal Sailors Rest, 69, 78, 181
Royal William Victualling Yard, 26

Saint-Nazaire, 44
Salcombe, 134, 136, 142, 151, 173, 196
Salisbury Plain, 144
Salute the Soldier Week, 166, 171–2,
Salvage workers, 85, 87–8, 137
Salvation Army, 76, 91, 116, 118, 143
Salvation Army Sailors Home, 143
Sandbags, 9, 17–19, 122
Scapa Flow, 21
Schuhart, Captain Lieutenant Otto, 14
Seahorse, 31
Seaton, 18
Sicily, 151–2
Sidmouth, 31, 34, 120, 132–3,
Sidmouth, HMS, 120
Simon, Sir John, 14, 36
Slapton Ley, 34
Slapton Sands, 159, 165
Softball team, 147
Southampton, 44, 55, 61, 114
Southampton Police Force, 61
South Atlantic, 26, 31, 34
South Brent, 121
Southern Command, 107
Southern Railway, 32, 66, 105, 161, 183
Southern Railway Orphanage, 161
Special constables, 13
Spitfire, 106, 129
Spooners and Co, 19, 94, 142
St Andrew's Church, 36, 67–8, 73–4,
    136, 182, 191
Starfish, 31
Stars and Stripes, 136
St Budeaux, 51, 53, 76, 113, 139
St David's Church, 30
St Paul's Cathedral, 53
Stephens, Alderman S., 17, 119
St Helier, 44
St Helier, 54
St John's Ambulance Association, 45
Stonehouse, 19–20, 50, 52, 62, 65, 67,
    76, 112, 141, 161, 187
Stonehouse Town Hall, 19, 65

Sugar duty, 14
Sutton Harbour, 30

Tamerton Creek, 37
Tanks for Attack campaign, 132
Tavistock, 31, 54, 56, 59, 106, 109, 118,
    125, 128, 136, 143, 163, 183, 194,
    197
Tavistock Fire Brigade, 106
Tavistock Scrap Metal Week, 125
Territorial Army Nursing Service, 16
Three Towns Club, 143
Three Towns Window Cleaning
    Company, 19
Tin Pan Alley, 149
Titanic, RMS, 44
Tobacco duty, 14
Torbay, 14, 34, 116, 176
Toronto, 119
Torquay, 9–11, 14, 29, 50, 109–10, 116,
    119, 127, 129, 140, 147, 152, 158,
    164, 175
Turnchapel, 42, 55–7, 155, 172

U-48, 52
U-94, 63
U-boat, 21, 192
Under Secretary for Air, 142
Undine, 31
United States Army, 136, 151–2,
    159–60, 164, 166, 179–80, 197
United States Navy, 112, 143, 167, 177
University College of the South
    West, 30
Utah beach, 159–60, 173

VE Day, 102, 187–9
Vegetarians, 31
VJ Day, 197

WAEC, 161
War Agricultural Committee, 105, 114,
    148, 151, 164

War Aid Supply Depot, 15, 19
War Emergency Order, 18
War Office, 15
War Savings Committee, 121
War Weapons week, 82, 100, 103, 106
Warner's Holiday Camps, 18
West Country, 7, 11, 14, 16, 21, 31, 36, 38, 45, 52, 103, 112, 116–17, 123–4, 142, 146, 173, 185
Weston Mill cemetery, 147
West Wales, SS, 63
Weygand, General, 46
Wings for Victory, 146
Wolsdon Street bomb, 62

Woolacombe, 152
Woolworths, 149
Women's Institute, 20, 165
Women's Voluntary Service, 15, 22–3, 29, 66, 85, 88, 98, 118, 136, 171–2, 176
Wonford Sessions, 22
WRNS, 123, 129, 147

Yelverton, 1, 10, 105, 110–11
YMCA, 132–3, 135, 181
Young Farmers of Winkleigh, 161

Zoo, 51, 122, 186